Andy Soutter was born in London in 1950 and educated at George Eliot School, Woolverstone Hall and Dartington College of Arts. His work has appeared in *Gay News*, *Interzone*, *PEN New Fiction*, *Performance*, *Skin Two* and *Rapid Eye*. His novel *Scrapyard* has been described as the first children's book to mention Nietzsche.

also by Andy Soutter

THE DRIVE-THRU MUSEUM:
A Journey Across The Everyday USA

for children

SCRAPYARD

AUSTRALIAVILLE
souvenirs of post-civilisation

Andy Soutter

An *Abacus* Book

First published in Great Britain in 1996
by Abacus

Reprinted 1996

Copyright © Andy Soutter 1996

The moral right of the author has been asserted.

A CIP catalogue record for this book
is available from the British Library.

ISBN 0 349 10718 1

Typeset by Solidus (Bristol) Limited

Printed and bound in Great Britain by
Clays Ltd, St Ives plc

Abacus
A Division of
Little, Brown and Company (UK)
Brettenham House
Lancaster Place
London WC2E 7EN

contents

contents

'Go away'

Aboriginal saying,
New South Wales, *c.* 1788

'As civilisation advances,
poetry almost necessarily declines.'
Essay on Milton,
Thomas Babington Macauley

One of Australia's contributions to the vanguard of the post-civil is the suburbs. They build them anywhere. They don't need to be attached to any city. Preferably, they put them down in the middle of some pastureland near the ocean. They need no town, no village; they have the global one at the push of a button. But suburbs *are* villages, and as such predate the urban and the civil. Much of the post-civil borrows from the pre-civil, so much that sometimes it looks like a reversion. It certainly resembles an escape.

The future is a suburb. It is also nomadic, feminist, psychedelic, part-time, aliterate, sexually diverse, ecological, areligious, sophisticated and communicative. It hasn't been like this since the Stone Age.

For the moment all it amounts to is a few bizarre plants poking through the rubble of contemporary derelictions, and their growth is not at all even. In one city lesbians can be officially married; in another they are more likely to be prosecuted. Here, therapy is shamanistic; there, electroconvulsive. It's enough to make Brigit ill: she has lost her meaning, like her sister Sheila. And, like Australia, she has suffered the violence of a civilised upbringing.

Here is a continent that has jumped from palaeolithic to post-industrial in just two hundred years. The speed of this recapitulation has left it with copious living remains of every stage, from the hunter-gatherers through each successive stage of civility to today's post-civilised people who sit in the suburbs wired to the globe, high on psychedelics, time on their hands, travel on their minds, Yothu Yindi T-shirts on their backs, Greenpeace stickers on their cars.

In Australia, shaman, farmer, industrialist, imperialist and republican pass each other on the street. Taxicabs go dreaming and palaeolithics present ballets. The urbane yearn for the countryside; farmers want to be nomads; nomads want service at the bottle shop, which may be owned by an erstwhile peasant. Priestesses are ordained as Ishtar twitches in her long coma. Leisure and sport and erotics intertwine; as skin cancer rains through an industrial-gauge hole in the sky, polychrome zinc warpaint appears and the whites go tribal, colourful as carcinomas. Past, present and future intermingle, clash, inter-marry, make mutations.

The most significant cultural divide today may be that between the civilised and prehistoric peoples of the world. In the light of this chasm, many of today's national, ethnic and racial conflicts, often between contestants sharing the same god and the same language, appear trivial by comparison. Civil-isation is *mono*cultural by nature. It is nervous about pronouncing that *other* word. In the face of post-civilised resurgences it hangs grimly on; it deals out its special opiates (you know them all by now) and turns ugly. It becomes Gilgamesh, sat in Uruk, a worried look on his face. He's still here, but the clocks are running backwards. Ishtar just twitched again. People are leaving the citadel for the villages. Farmers are heading for the hills. And there are some angry hunter-gatherers approaching, asking for their land back.

In the movie they made of Graham Greene's *Brighton Rock*, young Dickie Attenborough played Pinkie Brown, perfect for the teenage psychokiller role with his twitches and his wide-set eyes; and William Hartnell (face like a bloodhound, always old, born old[1]) was his henchman: provincial spivs in double-breasted pinstripe who wend their pathological way amongst sun, sea, pebbles and pleasure-seekers as they service their empire of gambling and protection rackets. This is a world where business competition is cut-throat (razors is one of the biznesses), ambitious men strut their stuff in slums and grand hotels, and the line between commerce and crime is blurred. A world where bent lawyers get drunk on 'Empire Burgundy'; and a psycho's world, Pinkie's world, of kitsch religious and other sadomasochistic fantasies, and of murder most foul at the pier funfair.

The story would have worked even better set in Sydney. Luna Park funfair is closed and decaying now, just like Brighton's West Pier, but good times, lotteries and *buers* are still high on the menu and the flavour of the mid-century still lingers on the streets where you can see period Morrises and

---

[1] Some twenty years on Hartnell was so old he qualified for eternity and so ended up playing the sci-fi timelord Dr Who.

schoolchildren dressed in uniforms of sixty years ago; while the power suits and padded shoulders of their elders also recall days long past (as well as the eighties), and there is plenty of old-time religion for them that needs it.

As for the spivs – this part of the world has always been famous for them, and this year there has been in Sydney and nationwide an even greater number of Pinkies caught with exposed porkies. Businessman Alan Bond has just been put behind bars; half of 'W.A. Inc.', the state government based in Perth, is on trial in the west; and in New South Wales the anti-corruption commission has just investigated and toppled the very man who established it, State Premier Greiner, who claimed he had been 'stabbed in the back'. Killings more literal than business scams and political demises also abound, from the series of rich old women murdered in Mosman to the Strathfield Massacre, to the more quotidian rapes, robberies and domestics.

Sydney Rock: sweet, cheap and sticky; sunny days and tabloid papers; arcades swimming in the odours of fast foods; armed robbery; tax evasion; road deaths on a par with pre-MOT Britain; racecourses, dogtracks; men with gaunt, lined faces and that grim William Hartnell expression. Just as Brighton has its bizarre Pavilion, Sydney has it own famous folly, the Opera House, a fantasy that has generated enough nicknames and similes (inventing these is a highly competitive national pastime) to fill a whole new extension of the Mitchell Library. Plenty of roast lamb and heavy cigarette consumption return us again to a previous Britain, as does the ample supply of rented homes and the casual, upfront racism.

And there's another echo: Bob Hawke is dethroned now but still in view parading the airwaves, the silver-quiffed Teddy Boy par excellence. Add a pair of brothel creepers, give him a cardboard trilby with the legend 'I AM A VIRGIN islander' and he wouldn't look out of place on any English south-coast seafront.

Down at Bondi you can walk the streets and run the gamut of that same south coast: Hastings Parade, Dover Heights, Ramsgate Parade ... amidst this year-round ultraviolet glare they have chosen to ennoble the memory of far away inside-if-wet signs, steamed-up tearooms and grey, gale-lashed promenades ... and Brighton Boulevard, Mother of Boulevards, narrow as a lane, pot-holed, classless – fancy apartment blocks and barrack-like council housing, flaking wooden bungalows alongside solid forties jobs of redbrick and pantile, Mercedes, beat-up Toyotas, Minis, old motorbikes – and practically treeless. A street doing its level best to mimic the conditions of the British southern littoral, Brighton Boulevard looks ordinary enough on a normal sunny Sydney day; you have to see it through a chilling sea-mist, on a rare day of cold and drizzle when the smell of fish and chips hangs longer in the air and you can hear boredom whingeing like that dog left out to skulk on the porch – now the street has come into its own and is worthy of its name.

How are they passing the time behind those unnaturally steamed-up windows? Maybe they're reading the words of Hawke's successor, the double-breasted (some say two-faced) Keating, who played Brutus to Bob's Caesar. In political debate Keating has a limitless supply of ear-catching appellatives, and these have just been collected in a book. The hundreds of character assessments run the gamut of emotions, from *ratbag* to *scumbag* and back again. Keating's a bruiser, born on the humble side of the tracks, like Pinkie Brown.

Sydney Rock, this store of quick energy, this bloody barber's pole, is a weapon as blunt as the PM's charming lexicography of slander; but splintered, sharp as an assassin's dagger. Pinkie also likes the cut and thrust, the vitriol of debate: he uses razorblades, and keeps a bottle of H_2SO_4 in his suit pocket.

A weapon, but also a comforter, sweet and pink as a religious promise. 'Quoting' St Paul, the church at Kirribilli offers you a FREE GIFT of eternal life; the hope of self-preservation as if in the solid sugar of Sydney Rock: and this mingles uncomfortably with paradoxic implications of decay, of rotting roots and putrefying cavities, of substance abuse, of obesity and pimples, candyfloss and bad breath, mood-swings, belligerence, bulimia; all the fun of the fair – perhaps eternal life is like this! The thumping echo of lurid pop tunes, the roar of the dodgems, the candy-striped poles, the helter-skelter ... and the blind accordionist-who-isn't-really-blind, the pickpockets, the spivs: sharpsuiters hustling innocents into the ghost train; collecting kickbacks in the merry-go-round's cabin ... down an alley between two tent shows lies a body oozing life while a polished political heel sneaks away around the corner, oblivious merrymakers kiss and clutch soft toys and wait transfixed as the tombola spins; while another snap-brimmed hood watches from the distance, leaning against the entrance to the tunnel of love, filing his nails.

At the end of *Brighton Rock* Pinkie gets his just deserts, and does himself in (H_2SO_4 steams up his face). His godfearing young moll believes that he has gone to Hell. He has not. Neither has he gone to Heaven. No chance. When Pinkie went down he went so far under he came out the other side. When Pinkie died, God – the fixer of the great lottery of life, the man who put the TAB[2] in ESTABLISHMENT, the ALE in NEW SOUTH WALES, the SEMEN in AMUSEMENT, and the HIGH RATE OF in LOCAL TEENAGE SUICIDE –God sent him straight to Sydney.

---

[2] State-run betting shops.

The first Australian I ever met transported me. She was a young woman with a soft, clear voice. Her vowels were peculiar and wonderful. Her face is a haze of faulty recall, but when she spoke she floated me off into an unforgettable ecstasy. I never listened to her sense. I was adrift on a sea of rhythms and vocalisations more powerful than any music I had ever known.

Did she know she was making love to me, had turned the room into a vast orgone accumulator, and had caused a thousand-petalled lotus to flame out from the top of my head? She was a supply teacher in London, England, and I was a kid in a class of young infants, high on the erotics of sound.

Marie-Antoinette was next. Another visitor. She never took off her sunglasses; she would never have her picture taken. She both drunk and exuded rich, heavy liquors. She hated all talk, especially small talk.

All these memories relate to sex and drugs ... buying hash at Earl's Court; meeting the gaunt blond editor of *Oz* magazine ... okkers in drunken Kent, hop-picking, driving tractors into the river at Goudhurst; inebriation and tortured metal, as was the case with a neighbour in Devon, a lagered-up trumpet student called Bruce.

One of the strongest drugs was a quick-acting barbiturate administered to me by two Australians in pale green hats and robes. The hospital room was like the deck of a starship. There was no better, faster assisted passage. I was down under in seconds.

This three-second barbiturate was arguably the most powerful drug – but that instant fix was in fact the strongest. It was the voice, a powerful intoxicant that may even produce endorphins in the manner of an opiate or a yogic exercise.

The English use many words but few vowels. Other nations with smaller vocabularies have a correspondingly wider range of sounds, like Norway's vast collection of a-e-i-o-u's. Australians speak English, but don't go in for the English habit of swallowing dictionaries. It may be that this makes them vowel specialists. Many Brits take an arrogant line on this and describe their speech as twisted, contorted or strangulated. But the English have never been much good at singing. The Australian voice is closer to song. And Australian people adore opera.

And the first Australians – didn't they *sing* their land into being? They came out of the ground, they walked and they sang: Tamarama, Woolloomooloo, Cooeeimbardi, Toogoolawah . . . travelling rhythms, saturated in vowels.

Later Australians sang in their version of the country with a class-conscious tale of the outback, a bizarre celebration of the waltz in 4/4 time. The swagman, like the earlier Ancestors, named the totem animal, then went back into the earth. But his voice remained, and may be heard as you pass by . . .

The first Australian I met in Australia was Aboriginal. She checked my passport and let me in. I liked that.

When I drove a cab around Sydney immersed in Australian voices, the radio operators were the principal, non-stop soloists. . . . The white Falcon emerged from its subterranean base at dawn and spent the rest of the day singing a thousand square miles into existence: Ghinagulla, Dee Why, Birriga and

the first australians

Bennelong; Hereford, Drummoyne, Wollstonecraft and Parramatta; Woomera and Waratah, Bent and Macquarie; Liverpool, Auburn, Leichhardt, Cronulla ... this taxi, this singing Ancestor, was a greater being than I. I had no control over it. Its voice dictated my directions, and it took me where it pleased. In front of the wheel, I was merely along for the ride, mesmerised. I could have been sitting at that infant school desk again, listening to that first Australian.

The most beautiful view in Sydney: the swathes of old industrial land at Rozelle/Balmain/Lilyfield, chaotic skeletons of redundant purpose, power station, railway yard, twisted steel, demolition sites, roadworks, temporary fencing.

Old Luna Park at Milson's Point: a dead fairyland, locked up and guarded with the rigor mortis of a security firm. How many princesses still imprisoned in those fabulous turrets? The pair of gateposts are painted with a giant declaration: HA HA. It's like a FUCK YOU.

Other inner city suburbs, a long time moribund, wait for the decision: demolition or gentrification – the stake or the revamp.

An old woman's protest in her front window: the wobbly crayon manifesto insists Keep Our Flag, We Dide For It, etc., etc.

Marc Camille Chaimowicz, a performance artist, said he aimed to create the impression that something had just happened, or was about to happen. He created romantic derelictions, scattered with candles and mirrors.

Dereliction, between the old and the new, lifts a place out of the continuum. Out of time, in the realm of myth. Free to accommodate the unspeakable. Examples: the forsakenesque ideal of gothick churches; Speer's 'ruin value'.

derelictions

Free to house the wildest of figures and schemes: Bennelong Point in the early sixties lies fallow, under a battle of competing designs for the Opera House.

A dereliction is a crossroads. Suicides are buried here, stuck between death and rebirth.

Just happened, or about to happen. A dereliction is a collection of questions and choices: what happened here? What happened to them? What will happen? Why? What is this place? Who is this person? What will I become, here? Should I? Shall we? Can I? Who am I? What do I want?

Factions fight over the future of derelictions, whether places or persons. Religions contest significant spots, agencies offer therapies and free soup and methadone and computer dating. How will the derelict be made to start anew? What shall we build on the deserted tracks? How shall we lift her depression? What drugs shall we use . . . ?

Where might we put the sofa, how would we fix the bathroom, in this empty bungalow, deserted apartment, cork-lined bedroom . . . ?

'I wonder who lived here . . . ?' What lives they led, what clues we can find.

You can always tell instantly. It's in the air, way before solid clues appear. You open the doors of some empty places and feel suspended joys rush out like a gale, else you step into heavy, greasy fogs of past disasters.

Derelict like a swollen skip, a receptacle of the forsaken. Things left behind, priceless or shitty (and the previous occupant's values were never yours).

Derelict like a satisifed lover, like the sleep of the juiced-out, like Candy Darling between parties.

Derelict like today, Halloween, the Celtic Samhain, the boundary between seasons, a no-man's land like the green line in Nicosia, a ghost town. Here be witches and warlocks, black and white, a summons of furies, an assault of fears, terrible reminders, female power unlocked: a woman on a winged phallus flies past the moon; tombs burst open; what you see is what you get – until it shape-shifts. Wild figures, wild schemes, wild speculations.

We are checking out an apartment in a sixties block on the headland at the south end of Bondi Beach. Light, airy, venetian blinds, parquet floor. On the balcony, last summer's fat on the barbie grill. Unfurnished but for a bentwood dining suite, and a bed in each back room. The atmosphere is ambiguous: faint scents of joy mingled with a vague, glutinous inference of defeat. The previous occupant's mail suggests a young Englishman whose mother is a TV actress in LA, and whose girlfriend has just walked out on him.

'Do we want to live in Bondi? Do we want ocean views? Can we live with that bit of damp wall? Can we live with mirror-door wardrobes?' says Brigit, then: 'He probably sold coke. They like mirrors.'

Experimenting with the position of the bed we lifted the mattress and discovered a small cache of pornographic magazines, a derelicted bundle. *Private* – photo sequences of various styles of heterosexual coupling (the men in the group scenes don't touch each other). Sperm is flying everywhere. I was turned on by a tall German woman with freckled tits and heavy thighs; Brigit got off on scenes of a Catholic priest's corruption via the mouth of a ponytailed adolescent. In one of these issues, the member of parliament for Rome (Lazio), Ms Ilona Staller, who is also a porn star and who regularly editorialises for *Private*, presented an open letter to the Pope in which she accused him of dereliction of duty; she attacked the man for his irresponsibility in not sanctioning condoms in the face of the AIDS epidemic. These columns of print were separated by charming photos of the writer (who is known as La Cicciolina) straddling a particularly beautiful phallus. I hoped the Pope had seen it. 'I'm sure he subscribes,' said Brigit. And here is how La Cicciolina describes her political aims:

'I am for a safe future without nuclear energy, for absolute sexual freedom, for the right to sex in prisons, against the death penalty, against all forms of violence, and for the decriminalisation of drugs. I am against censorship of any kind, in favour of sex education in schools, and for objective information about AIDS. In politics I have always spoken with love about human needs, in line with my socialist convictions.'

It's no surprise to learn that, despite the fact of her marriage to an American, the USA refuses her an entry visa.

Magazines like *Private* are of far greater value than anything pushed by Murdoch, Conrad Black and their ilk. An editorial like Staller's is worth a thousand leaders in the *Telegraph Mirror* and is the intellectual match for anything in *The Australian* or the *Sydney Morning Herald*; and the features displayed no trace of the endemic hypocrisies of mass media. Like all restricted, controlled or prohibited enterprises (nuclear power, chemicals, drugs), pornography is more inclined to exploit its workers and consumers and to push a proportion of dodgy material — but this is more like an argument for *freeing* the market in personal needs and pleasures, victimless pursuits like taking opiates or making love. What we do with our own bodies is not the business of any proselytising moraliser advancing behind a miasma of scientific half-truths and downright lies. (What the nuclear, chemical, armaments and psychiatric industries do to our bodies with their massive environmental poisoning is also our business, and we have a right to refuse these aggressions.) The issue is corporeal autonomy. For hundreds of years we have derelicted our rights to sexual pleasures; just as, since the turn of the century, we have increasingly derelicted our rights to buy and consume whatever drugs we choose. We are now in danger of vacating our bodies entirely and letting the state take up residence there.

I could feel my hard-on keeping the state at bay, staving it off.

We didn't take the flat, but we took the mags. Meanwhile we are renting a room from Anna Nassauer, who is an ex of Brigit's cousin Phil, in her small flat up on the hill behind Bondi Beach. Anna works in radio and teaches English to immigrants. She's a Bondi girl. Her father came over from Poland in the forties and still lives down the hill. Anna is tall and has a mass of jet-black hair, and a deep, lazy voice. She has a pastel-furnished living room with a matt-black TV and sound system, a pink oval answering machine, and a dusty Spanish guitar with a broken D string. The place always smells of Lavazza. Beyond the big metal-frame windows are rooftops and an inverted triangle of blue ocean and below the windows kids play hide-and-seek in the next-door garden and count up to twenty in a mixture of English and Russian. Anna does an easy three-day week. She drives a '78 Toyota and likes to weekend in the Blue Mountains or else go hang out down on the beach here. She's a little melancholy at the moment – a little derelict – on account of recently splitting up with an Israeli boy. Entering this sixties unit on lush Birriga Road is like stepping into a Helen Garner story. There is a quiet, organised sort of lassitude in the air. An unreal precision about things which extends to the way in which a newspaper has fallen from the arm of the sofa and configured itself next to a tiny green ashtray.

Brigit has been disturbed from day one here by the strong facial resemblance Anna bears to an ex of mine. 'Why don't you just screw her and get it over with?' she says desperately. 'It's quite obvious that you two are just itching to get it on.'

14

'She doesn't attract me,' I say, 'and you can be sure it's mutual. In another time and place, perhaps.'

'But she's beautiful.'

'So are you. So what?'

Brigit doesn't feel beautiful, although the pornography helps restore some of her confidence. This is partly because the models are quite unidealised, they come in all shapes, sizes and races. It stimulates sessions of sexual burlesqueries, of varying degrees of success.

'I'm not a dyke am I?' she says, tightening a leather belt around her bare midriff. 'Why am I so afraid sometimes? I know I'm not lesbian. It's not like I haven't had the chance.'

'I want to be sexual like this all the time,' she says, '– more than this – you haven't seen half of it, boy – but I'm so scared of what I'd let loose, I've got *so much power* inside me.'

'I thought it was men who were afraid of the dark and savage powers of unleashed female lust.'

'Yeah, and they're good at passing on the fear. Thanks, Daddy,' she said bitterly, 'for projecting all your own self-loathing onto me.'

'Got it.'

'Big deal. I can analyse till I'm blue in the face but makes no difference.'

Firecrackers burst from next door's Halloween party.

Then she speculates: 'I wonder if he *sexually* abused me?'

Brigit's beauty tonight is that of a bombsite in early spring.

Bondi Junction: if shopping in thirty-degree heat becomes a strain, you can always go to one of the masseuses in the Oxford Street mall, where they sit waiting on fold-up stools in front of some non-functioning shop window, young Thai men or white women who will knead you loose for a couple of bucks. And while you're being done you can bend your ears to a simultaneous selection of tunes coming from the numerous buskers who regularly populate this precinct. At this time of year there's a single theme. A small choir of school-children is singing 'In the Deep Midwinter'; a violin-and-brass ensemble is doing 'Once In Royal David's City'; the fat, mawkish Maori stands in front of his 100-watt karaoke system crooning out, à la Elvis, 'It'll Be Lonely This Christmas'. The punters, dressed for the beach and the surf, amble from shop to shop or sit on benches beneath small plane trees, smoking, snacking, devouring ice creams; and their carrier bags are printed with holly designs or pictures of Santa Claus and his reindeer dashing through the snow. Further off at the Bondi Road junction the two leggy blonde girls in wet T-shirts and cut-off shorts who hustle with bucket and sponge, screenwashing at the traffic lights, have red-and-white Santa hats perched at rakish angles, and are doing excellent business: a dollar cleans your screen and gives you a good perv at the same time.

Meanwhile, the media abound with warnings about skin

cancer from this violent southern sun; bush fires are raging north of the city; and in the west of the state drought is decimating cattle stocks and helping clog up the Darling River with pernicious blue-green algae. Soon it will be the long summer vacation, and an endless round of cricket, tennis, barbies and beach parties. What better time to celebrate a midwinter festival?

Christmas Day, North Bondi: we're in Brigit's cousin Trish's flat above a row of shops where the buses terminate. Phil's here, so is Aunt Jean, long widowed, and her other son David, twenty-eight, water on what appears to be an unusually large brain, 'mental age' of eleven. We have turkey, cabbage, parsnips, gravy and all the trimmings, sat on sofas around a low table in front of the TV, where Max Bygraves is doing his stuff. It's stifling in this tiny living room, and what little breeze floats through the net curtains is even hotter than the steamy atmosphere inside. Modest presents are exchanged: chocolates, fancy cigarettes, AUSTRALIA T-shirts, ball-point pens emblazoned with Sydney University's coat of arms . . . David has been given a Judith Durham record and booms out his approval in a voice like a sledgehammer before bursting into song: 'THERE'S A NEW WORLD SOMEWHERE, THEY CALL THE PROMISED LAND . . .', all the verses, word-perfect. The air is blue with the many cigarettes smoked before, during and after the meal. Trish's face is grey from years of tobacco addiction and office work; Jean's perm is a brilliant platinum; Phil's nicotine-stained fingers lovingly handle his mother's present of a Miles Davis CD. 'PHIL, HAVE YOU SEEN STARLIGHT EXPRESS YET?' enquires David, whose mum takes him to every show in town. 'No, mate,' smiles Phil. 'WHAT STAR SIGN ARE YOU, BRIGIT?' says David, and she tells him. 'WHAT STAR SIGN ARE YOU?' he asks me, and I tell him. 'DANGER, DANGER!' says David, and he means it. He backs away from me: 'INCOMPATIBLE!' (David's a

Virgo; I'm a nomad invader, hooves thundering, bow drawn.)

By the time Brigit and I take our leave Max has given way to a carol service and David has sung-along with every pious tune. Now he has been distracted by his mother's arms. 'YOU'VE GOT CARCINOMAS, MUM – DANGER! DANGER!'

'No, darling, they're liver spots,' says Jean.

Brigit and I walk down to Bondi Beach. The last time I saw so much concrete was in the middle of Berlin. Here, it looks like a war is about to start and all that's missing is the razorwire. There's the wide curving swathe of road, Campbell Parade, which looks like the foundations of some heavy-industrial development, the razed remains of a recession-hit factory, weeds in the cracks, cement blocks strewn about to divert traffic. And there are concrete footbridges, cracking and closed, and paths and little blockhouses, and across a stretch of knackered grass is the sea wall and promenade, a vast betonic bulwark which could keep out the combined navies of the world riding in on a tidal wave. This place looks like some disused airfield only recently reclaimed by its inhabitants, who are still figuring out exactly what to do with it. At present it makes a barrack ground look exotic. Its glory is crowned at night by the sewage stack high up on the headland, which has been wreathed in sparkling lights which transform it into an enormous dazzling champagne glass spraying silver bubbles into the midnight sky. This afternoon the beach itself has become an ocean of fluttering Union Jacks. Packed together in little groups, the Brits in their thousands have taken it over, each group with its home town blazed across the flag's centre bar: NORTHAMPTON, LEICESTER, BELFAST, NEWCASTLE-UPON-TYNE. Here are roast limbs with all the trimmings. The beer flows, and on the sea wall a hefty sound system pumps out disco for the thick throng of dancers.

June, Katoomba: yesterday we were roasting in the outback,

but here at 3000 feet up in the Blue Mountains it's close to freezing, and I'm shivering in my denim jacket, below a giant banner which arches over the main street. It reads YULE FESTIVAL.

In this country you can throw seasonal rhythms to the wind and watch them form patterns of displacement and dislocation, discrepancy and sudden change, although there's nothing inexplicable about the British takeover of Bondi Beach on Christmas Day. This day is about links with 'the old country', which is why they send off, from burning Perth or tropical Queensland, seasonal aerogrammes with fir-trees-and-snow designs for the information of their European relatives. Plenty of them have never seen snow; plenty more love these wonderful discrepancies, which are all part of a life marked by peculiar importations: every kind of foreign product, festival, folkway and religious habit, and all sorts of differing cultural cues. Serbs and Croats at loggerheads in Melbourne; in-fighting Iranians busting up Canberra; Turks making anti-German demonstrations. They'll use anything here: an Aboriginal dance troupe mixes in ballet with its show; and a commercial for the latest Holden proudly proclaims that the car is 'Fully Imported'.

Katoomba is a quiet town, like somewhere on the edge of a Devon moor. Its high street offers wholefoods, books, Fair Isle knitwear, Drizabone waxed coats. Noticeboards advertise practitioners of various brands of neo-shamanism. Although we caught none of the festivities during our overnight stay, it appeared that the Katoombans had organised themselves something strange for Australia: a phenomenon that was practically organic, homegrown; archaic, yet apt: a midwinter festival at the appropriate time of year, and one uncorrupted by notions of Christianity or beach volleyball.

'A sweet disorder in the dress
Kindles in clothes a wantonness ...
A careless shoe-string, in whose tie
I see a wild civility
Do more bewitch me, than when Art
Is too precise in every part.'

'Delight in Disorder', Robert Herrick

A certain strange object can be seen daily making its way around the central business district, else parked up in some suburb. It is a small grey panel van with no rear windows and two tiny ones at the side. Its flat panels, rivets and square construction give it the appearance of a security truck, an armoured personnel carrier. On its sides is painted a single word ALARMS, followed by a phone number. Across its rear end is emblazoned the following: British Ultra Loyalist League Serving Historic Interests Today. The first letter of each word is writ large, so the acronym BULLSHIT stands out a mile away. And one of the side windows is blinded with a picture of the Princess of Wales.

Alarms. Bullshit. British interests. A small grey armoured vehicle. Princess Diana. Who is responsible for spreading this oblique message? Is it a dream of Ned Kelly roaming the city with a display of ironic theatrics? Has he learned that the sublime is indestructible?

Or is it a portrait, in the Nolan style, of the last of Empire? The last prison van, the old guard. A hulk. A dumb-cell. Are there prisoners inside, or are there the besieged ghosts of old governors – a silk-clad huddle of baroque psychopaths reading the *Daily Telegraph Weekly*: Macquarie and Menzies and Marsden – and has this surreal intervention become their tumbrel?

Questions, questions. Alarums and excursions.

NOT THE FIRST FLEET BUT THE BEST FLEET says the sign on the door. This small room – low ceiling, white walls, grey carpet – has about fifty people crammed into its ranks of black plastic stacking chairs. Predominant dress: marblewash denim, the universal immigrant's uniform. Predominant gender: male (there's one woman). Predominant language: hard to say; at a pinch English might just get a working majority, but not as a mother tongue – this would be Chinese or Thai. Other mothers in contention here would be Levantine, Greek, Gujarati, Russian, Maori, Polish, Serbo-Croat, Vietnamese, Chileno, Farsi.

But as far as nationalities are concerned we are all supposed to share just the one. It is a bureaucratic nationality, an abstract affair, a cluster of bytes, a frame around a blank piece of paper. This frame is not symmetrical – it is an outline logotype of the national map, a badge so ubiquitous, adorning the public image of nearly every public and private enterprise, saturating TV and print media with its horn and its bulges, that it implies a constant need for people to orientate themselves. You Are Here, says the plan-silhouette of the continent, somewhere in the thousands of miles between Perth and Brisbane, Torres Strait and Tasmania, Adelaide and Darwin, somewhere on the biggest island you could conceive of. But this map works by default. It gives each person a specific reminder of where they are not – Assam, Ireland, Yugoslavia, etc. Its sister logo is just as apt: it shows an animal in flight, a fast animal, built for escape, lean, aerodynamic. This Is Your Totem. Consider the implications of this graphic one–two and the psychological impact it might make. Then take account of the third sister of the triad: the Southern Cross, glittering celestial torture instrument. Wherever you are you can always find the Southern Cross. Look up into the night sky: it's just to the south-east of the Union Jack.

No, we're certainly not the First Fleet. They were better dressed. And our own collective criminal record probably speaks of deeds far graver than the offences which sent the original convicts off in their brig-rigged sloop-to-Hell.

We are following the words – with some difficulty – of a stocky little man in his mid-thirties who is pacing up and down between blackboard and lectern. He wears shorts and a codpiece of a purse-belt. In his mélange of Mediterranean and South African English, Billy is lecturing on Personal Safety. It seems there was this Japanese driver who always carried nunchakus under his seat, and one night his passengers got out and ran off without paying; so what does our man do? He pursues them into a block of units wielding his chain sticks and gets stabbed to death for his trouble. Married with kids, this young Japanese. All the co-ops had a whip-round, gave him a good funeral – 'But what was it all for? Five bloody dollars, so you know what I mean, right?'

He means don't carry weapons, and don't follow hoods into housing projects. One's illegal, both could be suicidal. What – not even a little pistol, knife ... Mace, even? Jaws drop, eyes widen, apprehension reigns – 'How do we defend ourselves, mate?' We've all heard the horror stories. Media hype, says Billy, and rattles off some more comforting statistics. Nobody's comforted. 'But don't forget you got the tools of your trade, innit? You got to have a torch of course, and this is the torch you want—' And he delves into his bag and lifts out a heavy, chrome-plated two-foot-long rolled steel truncheon. 'Now this is not an offensive weapon,' he smiles. There's a ripple of appreciation and applause. 'Get yourself one of these,' advises Billy. 'And of course all drivers need a wheelbrace, don't they?' This is much more comforting than statistics. Now a question-and-answer session: what other tools might a driver need? Long screwdriver? – correct, good; long-nosed pliers – yes, good; tyre levers, big spanners … the inventory runs its comforting course. End of lecture.[1] We crowd out into the lobby of the Least-Cost Taxi School, where walls, ceilings and everything else which doesn't move is tanned with nicotine and the air is blue with smoke. Sydney colours: sky blue and beige.

I buy hot chocolate from the machine, pick out the little cockroach and step outside into the violent sunlight. Trucks and semi-trailers rumble past belching smoke. This is the main drag in Alexandria, a major route connecting downtown Sydney with the airport, light-industrial belt and container terminals at Port Botany. Across the narrow two-laned road, outside the Social Security offices, is a long queue of baby buggies and chainsmokers, whites, mixed race, Aboriginals, scuffing around in trainers. The lines of shops, two-storey nineteenth century affairs with heavy iron awnings, are grubby places selling cheap food, Chinese driving lessons, secondhand clothes, sweets, magazines, MSG and cigarettes. Real-estate agents are conspicuously absent. Most people live in the nearby clutch of high-rises, which along with the stark yellow-brick office building that houses the taxi school are the only modern

---

[1] Deleuze and Guattari, in *Nomadology* (Semiotext(e), 1986) offer some interesting speculations on the differences between the tool and the weapon.

structures in sight. Least-Cost also owns the video library on
the corner and have given me a plastic membership card. This
Alexandria is a centre of learning on a par with its classical
namesake.

Back inside, through the open door of another smoke-filled
room I can see the walls lined with computer screens, each
attended to by an earnest oriental face as lists of locations are
learned by rote. Then into the lecture room (the seats fill up
always from the back; the front row is shunned unless
unavoidable) to learn how to use a street index. I paid four
hundred dollars for this, along with units such as Diet &
Health, where you learn that fast food, saturated fats and
cigarettes are bad for you; and the preceding one on Personal
Safety in which Billy, in his white nylon shirt with slip-on
epaulettes proclaiming TAXIS COMBINED SERVICES, had
explained that cabbies were exempt from having to wear
seatbelts because it is too easy for Johnny Punter to use them as
a garrotte. However, the street-index exercises weren't simple
for most. Having passed quickly through this part of the tripos
I then spent half an hour trying to pass on my wisdom to a
young Thai who had three words of English (Please and Thank
You) while all around us worried faces pored over maps and
lists of incomprehensible names (Castlereagh, La Perouse,
Warringha, etc.). And within a week or two they could all quite
possibly be plying the streets, torches and wheelbraces at the
ready, doubtless praying for guidance from above, or below, or
wherever their particular lord and compass hung out.

This is Sydney's version of The Knowledge. One of the two
state-regulated schools through which an aspiring cabbie must
go to get his authority. The whole tamale – lectures, videos,
drama-docs on sexual and racial harassment, slide shows of
downtown Ramadas and Hiltons, medical, mugshot, three-
hour bus tour, ten-minute driving test – can be got through in

fourteen days. You're then allowed to ply around with your little amber roof light aglow amongst the five million people and thousand square miles of metropolis. You may have lived here for years, or you may have just arrived from Bangkok without even Please, Thank or You; it doesn't matter. All you need to be is Desperate. Taxi driving is the bottom line in this burgh. There are three thousand licensed cabs in Sydney and they're cheap to hire. And the last few years of economic wobblies have seen more and more cabs chasing fewer and fewer punters. It's Taxi City, and most of them are vacant. You only have to stand in the street and pick your nose to find seventeen fish-eyed six-cylinder Ford Falcon sedans swerving across lanes and squirming to a halt on all sides of you. Then watch the multicultural brawl break out. Cabbies' earnings are low and getting lower. They're insulted, duped, despised and attacked. They work what are known as 'unsocial' hours and survive on coffee, fags, and nerves shredded and woven into the pattern of a paranoid obsession with the dreamlines of a city. Yeah, this is the job for me.

Watching the NBC *Today* programme after midnight supplies the first sensations of time dislocated. It's yesterday morning in America. A reporter in a fur hat outside Bethlehem Steel talking about layoffs and recession. Then a jolly fat man, hat, coat and gloves against the blizzard, sending out birthday greetings sponsored by Hallmark to a series of tough old centenarians, all women, from Florida to Seattle, the screen suffused with their glowing pink faces. Yesterday morning in the American ice age. I fix iced coffee and crush a roach while crickets sing outside the window and an air-conditioner hums and drips in the window opposite. On the floor a horde of red ants plunders an almost empty bottle of Bondi Junction Cola (with added ginseng), and a busy two-lane ant highway stretches tidily around the skirting boards to the gap under the front door. At two-thirty the phone warbles twice and I step outside into the warm, sultry air and the sweet-shop scents of plant blossom. Descending to the street I face the dark gothic arches of the Opera House across the water. There's an orange glow over the city and the neon of downtown hotels is reflected in the harbour waters. Then there's a sharp tang of liquid petroleum gas from the exhaust of the cab waiting in the avenue.

The driver is a short bald Belgian. As we race over the bridge and along the spaghetti freeways of the Western Distributor he tells me he was a soldier in the Congo before it became Zaire. Then he'd come over here for the sunshine. Why hadn't he gone somewhere nearer like South Africa? – 'At that time you couldn't go with African women in SA. I had a lot of African wives: girls – virgins. There's nothing tighter than the cunt of an African virgin, and they're so cheap to buy. Every few months I divorce her, give her back to her parents and take another one. The cunt is so tight because they sew the lips up, you know?' His present wife is Maori.

Along deserted Goulburn Street (Chinatown ... Triple X raincoat cinema ... blind concrete monolith of the Masonic HQ) and into Surry Hills, a square kilometre of rolling slopes, one side of a much bigger hill. Streets: narrow. Buildings: Victorian terraced houses, small, two-storey'd; warehouses; whorehouses. Aka Scruffy Hills. Industries: print (News International, Reader's Digest ...), rag trade, rehab centres, methadone clinics; sweatshops all. Streetnames: Crown, Albion, Commonwealth, etc. Population: Chinese families, white musicians, winos, heroin users. Heavily forested with avenues of 100-year-old planes. 'Undeveloped': quaint but not yet cute; a period reservoir, a few stretches of cobbled street, colonial terraces barricaded by giant palm fronds. Shady.

The Legion base on Foveaux Street is a Bauhausy affair,

white concrete and cylindrical pillars; a slope leads down from street level to lines of gas pumps and a stream of cars coming in off the night shift. Drivers hang around in clutches, popping green cans of Victoria Bitter. Everybody is doing tobacco, from pump attendants to car-wash fellers clumping around in wellies and sodden shorts and T-shirts, who are hosing and smoking and sponging and calling out impatiently for cars to be collected: Triple Six! Triple Six! Get it out of here! Nobody comes for the Number of the Beast and I wonder if it's been earmarked for me, it might come in handy out there. Other drivers scuff around impatiently waiting for their cars to arrive, and when they do, bundle themselves and their belongings inside in seconds, expel the erstwhile driver, and hustle off out of there like the devil is on their tailpipe. The fleet manager is a fair-haired, pugnacious-looking being of French Canadian extraction called Eric Augé. He'd look even shorter if he didn't wear Cuban-heeled boots with winklepicker toes. He either acts concerned and pally, else stone-coldly, whichever way suits him at the time. He's pally tonight, but I don't get 666. He gives me an old maroon Falcon which carries a cancer research ad on the boot and inside stinks of cigarettes. Its name is 1915. It's heavy as a tank and there's no power steering. I re-christen it Gallipoli and haul it out into the street.

The world rushes in, into my living room ... it's like TV. I'm a talk-show host on wheels. I welcome them, I give the pissed and garrulous their head of steam, I moderate debates, I seduce intimate revelations from the shy, I counsel the confused. I let the insults roll off me (fuckin' pommy ... male pig ... taking jobs from our kind ...) and smile with equal grace at the compliments (at least he's not your slit-eyed chinko ... at least you're Anglo-Saxon ... I've let about twenty darkie-cabs go by ...). And I manipulate their moods with the appropriate music. Thelonius Monk works on everybody over the age of eighteen, and this club-sound implies – almost demands – a confessional or informative encounter. These taxis are intimate little saloons: there's no partition; our auras mingle, our eyes meet unmediated by mirrors. I tease them, please them, let them know I love them. I'll do anything for them – I'll drive to places remote, dark and bushy; I'll suffer the noxious perfumes of Double Bay women or the overpowering stink of non-scented soap as I am ruthlessly used by Christians and by Scientologists; the tedious prattle of stereotyped brains – racist, hypochondriac, boor, bore; the dull robotics of expatriate Englishmen; the Irish, double-crazy in the Antipodes; the vomiting, the violent and the drunk. They can fuck with me any way they please. I'm the whore with the heart of a gold-plated LED meter, and like the classier whores in this town I have a panic button close to hand, though I'll never have to use it. I imagine I can make myself immune to violence as if it were just a bacterium or some vile priestly philosophy.

My favourite customers are those tall Darlinghurst women: deep-voiced, sensual, slippery beings who take me from club to club and whose trip is to mimic male T/Vs: reality cubed. If I was rich I'd give all of these hyposurrealists a free ride. But they all pay. Even the Haitians from Blacktown – five adolescent Tontons Macoutes – handed over dollar bills before sneaking off with the change bag. The only ones who don't comply are the occasional uptight middle-class white girls too pissed to work the automatic tellers who swear to send ten dollars in the post and never do. Payment sometimes comes in US dollars, whisky or grass. Sex is rarely offered, which is just as well because it takes time and you can't cash the consequences. (But I'm still just a hooker on wheels, and at shift's end I'll hand over half my earnings to that Cuban-heeled Kanuck pimp.) Rich riders – power dressers flying out on Ansett, etc. – give the meanest tips, and the best come from lank-haired and tattooed greasers, sometime cabbies and other terminal sleazebags as desperate as myself, as well as bemused newcomers, timid country girls just off the Queensland bus who think that Sydney is the wildest place on earth and who have heard that cabbies will suck their blood if denied a 50 per cent pourboire. Schoolgirls, however, are always a dollar short of the fare; they brazenly expect this discount for raising the cab's pheromone level. (A cab is in fact an orgone box on wheels.) These pubescents come in full Angela Brazil, 1920s drag: district-nurse hats and pinafore slips; and the males, beefy and hairy from age twelve, are forced into caps and tailored shorts which makes them either ludicrous or horny according to taste. But the plain, loose style of the girls' dress gives them a peculiar grace. Another time and place dislocation is the occasional sight of such a child holding a bar of Cadbury's chocolate and climbing into a '51 Morris Minor. Always in Sydney this thin thread of imperial traffic – the Triumph Herald, the Rover 3000, the MG Magnette, the Wolseley 6/90, the Riley 1500, the Standard Vanguard, the Ford Zephyr, the Morris Major, the Land-Rover – picks its way through the heavy weave of Falcons, Holdens, Datsuns, Toyotas and Hondas. And always above them, a snot-yellow streak of smog bleeding into the incessant blue. Half this sulphur comes from cigarettes – the folks here burn their way through packs of twenty-five, thirty-five and fifty a day (the blond tobacco is dry and harsh and the brands have cheap names like Peter Jackson and Winfield – Woolworth's fags, the crud of the crop) as they bomb around town in Ford Dioxins and Honda Zyklons leaking lethal gas from every gaping pipe and busted gasket. Out in the rolling rurals of the upstate, the folks call Sydney 'Syanide'. Perhaps they long for the days of the First Fleet, when all there was to worry about was white deaths in custody and a bit of algae in the water.

Bob Dylan, who has always had a sideline in the wry and the dry, once wrote and recorded a song about a palm-tree'd luxury resort where a collection of appropriate characters – a thinly disguised Jackie Onassis (all *Vogue* and Panama hat), a croupier speaking cod French, a suicidal Greek, an obsequious desk clerk, a soldier looking to buy gold, a loser in the casino, and a closet homosexual – all run around stupidly in a flash hotel whilst collectively failing to heed the rumblings of a nearby volcano and a basement boiler. Finally it all blows up and they perish in disaster. Watching news of the catastrophe on TV, 'in LA watching old Cronkite', the narrator concludes with tired contempt that it's 'just another hard-luck story' and wanders off to the fridge for a beer.

Among other things, this song is a fine exposition of that phenomenon the South Americans call *pava* – the connection between bad taste and bad luck. Gabriel Garcia Marquez has referred to it as a jinx which attaches itself to pretentious people and objects. The song is called 'Black Diamond Bay'.

I had enjoyed that song for twenty years, but I had never come across Black Diamond Bay until the day I walked into Double Bay, which is on the south side of the harbour a couple of miles east of downtown Sydney. I already had a single clue to its reputation, culled from a Sydney University student magazine, in the spoof lonely hearts column, where a lovelorn correspondent was advertising for a merino ewe to make love to; failing that a tight-fitting fur-lined gumboot would suffice; and, in the last resort, 'a nice Double Bay girl would do'.

Double Bay shops sell stuff which has as little to do with survival as it has with beauty – in other words, expensive junk. Junk you'd find elsewhere in places such as the Burlington Arcade, or the quieter parts of a duty-free complex anywhere in the world. The place is bijou. Low-rise buildings, sidewalk cafés; the shopping streets are like catwalks. People here dress for the benefit of mirrors, of which there is a surfeit, in shops, in handbags, on sunglasses: reflective surfaces – cars, polished shopfronts, jewellery, cocktail bars – are everywhere. Double Bay shines, though it dazzles only itself. Toy dogs, spotless new four-wheel-drives, gear by Gucci and Country Road; G&Ts and Nuits D'Or in the sailing club lounge; and yet a peculiar tension is always evident: the women are bound by image, the men by muscle. It is a female environment in the same way that Hampstead Village is, or Golders Green. Soft beige leather and leopardskin ... you could even call it Double Bagel.

The Ritz Carlton is Double Bay's Camelot. A discreetly fronted low-rise building with a lot of polished marble guarded by beefy, red-faced and spotty young men in long coats and top hats, it houses the richest of the suburb's visitors. Its name is double-barrelled overkill; each word oozes pretension – for a century or more both have been widely used to hype up the trashiest of travel bags, cigarettes, saloon cars, cameras, stereos and chocolates ... this is *pava* territory. Take extreme care. Beware accidents.

I knew Double Bay had *pava* from the first, but what underlined this emphatically was the time George Bush put up there in the course of his election-year tour, as he desperately tried to drum up American business around the Pacific. This was the famous Dead Duck Tour, when he collapsed at that dinner in Japan; I'm convinced it was something he picked up in Double Bay, just as it is certain that he left some *pavaic* bacteria behind from the mutual and loving exchanges of contact with the fellow woodentops and fawning flunkies of the Ritz Carlton.

I used to get the odd bit of radio work out of this pub. The Ritz is the only place in town which will specify a 'clean' cab, or one that must have air-conditioning, or must have bucket seats; and they probably used the fleet I drove with because it had the smallest number of non-white drivers. My passengers were without exception ugly, inept, insecure and unfriendly; and their conversations always dwelt upon mishaps or crises. The sole occasion any of them ever left a tip was the sole occasion I ever refused one: they left the money on the seat and I tossed it out the window. Couldn't use it – that sort of money has *pava*. And I'd always known when a fare I picked up elsewhere was going to Double Bay: they would be female, overdressed and swathed in a cloud of poisonous scent. If there was more than one they'd be talking tights and hairdo's. 'So whereabouts in DB are you going?' I'd say before they could open their mouths, and if they got snotty I'd intimidate them with my Prince Charles accent. I had no tip to lose.

But *pava* rubs off. Too much contact pollutes. Marquez would move house if he found anyone on the same block with *pava*. I began to avoid Double Bay as much as possible and felt better as a result. Double Bay's luxurious patina is a brittle one; there are too many personal boilers ready to blow. It's only a matter of time before I find myself wandering off to the fridge for that mythical beer.

Geoff Beardmore is a big bloke in his forties with a shining bald pate. He wears a short-sleeved shirt, tailored shorts and knee-length socks. He's driving a minibusload of rookie cabbies on an afternoon tour of the city. We've just swooped down from North Sydney, where according to Geoff the girls are a bit wild: 'They won't keep their hands off you. All the clubs in North Sydney are like that. A bloke can't have a quiet drink with his mates.'

Now we're passing St Vincent's Hospital in Darlinghurst, and on the corner is the AIDS hospice. Now the good-natured Geoff turns a little surly: 'I don't know what's floating around in there,' he says, 'and I'm not going to find out.'

One in the eye for mankind's adventurous spirit.

It's a fine line between mateship and homoerotics, if indeed one exists at all. Some men are mates and some men mate. And some men will end up in St Vincent's Hospice, and so will some others.

With rugby league, that fine line comes close to dissolution. It's a beefed-up version of kiss chase, an orgy of fierce embraces. Those skimpy, satin-smooth nylon shorts are basically French knickers, and they are too provocative. The Great Britain side is touring this spring, and in match after match they cannot resist planting sudden kisses and giving those Aussie bums a friendly squeeze – and this leads to a furore in the media. It seems you can crack a fellow player's skull with impunity, whereas blowing a kiss is anathema.

I took a couple home one night from a North Sydney nightclub of the kind Geoff Beardmore (Geoff has a nice pair of legs) would stay well clear of. All the way to Lindfield they argued about rugby. This may seem a strange subject for two young lovers locked in amorous embrace in the back of a taxi, but is it really? Year by year now, along with all the concomitant bulky costumerie, sport is throwing off the pretensions of recent centuries: the notion that it is exclusively about honour (personal, local, national), courage, and the rather abstract 'achievement'; and a kind of pseudoscientific 'progress' (especially an indulgence in mensuration, listings and statistics, on a par with the achievements of train-spotters and *Mastermind* contestants) embodied in physical training and record-breaking. But now the erotics of sport are re-emerging, and we are approaching a situation reminiscent of images from classical Greece – the naked athlete. The naked athletes whose physical exercises (yogas) put them in an altered state of expanded consciousness (aerobicised, endorphinated, hyperventilated) similar to the orgiastic state experienced during skilled sexual intercourse (Tantrism, etc.). Indeed, athletic intercourse is often a prelude to coition. Lovers will wrestle as foreplay, and a good work-out always frees the libido.

Being both sexy and spectator-oriented, sport is by extension pornographic. In modern times the athlete has come out, shed her restrictive skirts and his inhibiting trousers and come more and more to resemble a contestant in a beauty contest or a nightclub dancer. Look at those Uncle Toby's Iron Men, their huge torsos emerging from the waves, those powerful thighs pumping, those tiny black G-strings, as they lope across the sand; check out the beach volleyball girls – you won't be the only one not watching the ball. Athletes are now porn stars to an audience of billions. Prepubescent Eastern European girls flaunt themselves on the bar in a reprise of every Victorian gentleman-photographer's fantasies; cue screaming women and creaming kecks as wrestlers grapple it out; cue lycra and spandex; cue *Gladiators*, a sex show which is a mischievous parody of the idea of sport-as-martial-art, as military training, as winning an empire from the playing fields of Eton: the combatants here dress like models in skin mags, give themselves exotic names like strippers do, and use soft toys as joke weapons, belabouring each other with giant cotton buds, bombarding each other with – ouch – tennis balls, throwing cushions around, hurling themselves down upon huge squidgy mattresses, limbs akimbo – and generally having a psychedelic pyjama party in front of an audience roaring lustily beneath the coloured lights. This is true decadence. Caligula himself would be outraged by *Gladiators*: this is not the Colosseum, this is the stuff of the End of the Empire, this is what saps moral fibre and enfeebles armies; cue also low-angle shots of leaping netball players, and piles of scrummaging men in flimsy camiknickers. Even the Olympians have been contaminated, viz. Ben Johnson, a hyped-up sperm shot from a gun, his taut leotard, prominent package and rippling buttocks bursting to a finish with a trail of white tape in his wake.

Sport's tension is between the erotic and the aggressive. In this dynamic of the sexual *v.* the martial – this fixture if you like – the former element has re-emerged with a vengeance after a long period of sublimation. Even American football – essentially a scenario of men at war on behalf of their women who support them from the sidelines – is now a cuddly affair: the players are fully protected, cocooned inside helmet and padding, and the artificial pitch is clean and unhazardous; the players' shoulders are emphatically wide, their crotches emphatically tight, and bottoms … oh, their bottoms … and their girls bump and grind, long legs and tinsel on the chorus line.[1] Is this how it all started, back in earliest Sumer – two men put on a sex show for the goddess, who will bed her favourite, the more virile, the one whose cock stays harder longer? And by the time men have taken power in the land, and are now making love to compete for ownership of the woman – it follows that a person whose willy won't work for him will resort to other means: a caress turns into a headlock, a knee thumps into the groin, and competitive sport is born.

My two passengers were still busy with their foreplay – arguing the comparative merits of rugby union versus rugby league – when I dropped them. The girl preferred union (it was faster, with more tactical variations), while her companion had just one word for union players, which he never stopped repeating: '*Softcocks*,' he said, 'that's all they are, bloody *softcocks*.'

---

[1] Thus, on Remembrance Sunday at the Cenotaph in London, the monarch and male royalty take part in the ceremony while the royal women watch from high up on a distant balcony. These ladies don't *appear* to be dancing, but on the other hand you can't see their feet.

In a quiet corner of the central business district near Circular Quay there stands a small memorial to the first Christian service to be held on Australian soil. It's worth noting that this event took place some days after the completed disembarkation from the convict ships in the cove. In fact it might appear that religious activity did not have a high priority during the first years of European colonisation. Catholic Christians had to wait over a decade until 1803 for their first authorised assembly, and Anglican priests did not begin to arrive in droves until later in the nineteenth century.

However, the budding colony did have a chief priest to preside over its formative years, and a notorious one at that. He was the Reverend Dr Samuel Marsden who, when he wasn't busy obtaining more and more land for himself to breed his sheep on, was busy women-hating (he set up the Female Register in which all women bar old widows were described as either 'married' or 'concubine' – just the two choices as usual, girls), and when he wasn't doing these things he was hard at work having convicts flayed in his capacity as Parramatta's magistrate. He was known as the Flogging Parson and Parson Rapine, and appears to have been as good an all-round sadist and bigot as the church has ever supplied. It is indicative of his popularity that when an arsonist destroyed Sydney's only

Anglican church, no one would grass on the culprit despite the carrot of a free pardon, free trip home and fifty pounds into the bargain. Just as well for Marsden that he preferred to do God's work outside this building as he made the rounds of New South Wales, torturing confessions from prisoners and lashing men and women to the triangle for two hundred strokes of the nine-tailed whip. Thus was the crucifix carried forth and the Christian Church established – if not particularly respected – in Australia.

I'm sitting under this memorial cross reading an article in the Australian edition of *Time* magazine by Robert Manne, a lecturer in politics at Melbourne's La Trobe University. According to Manne, we now live in a 'post-religious' society, and life is so much more depraved and violent as a consequence. The article is called 'Pornography and Mass Murder', and Manne is talking of psychopaths like Wade Frankum who recently made Strathfield – a dreary district in Sydney's west – even more dreary by gunning down a number of innocents in the Strathfield Mall. A brief biography tells us that Frankum bought material dealing with sex and violence, and got female prostitutes to bugger him with a dildo, and Manne concludes that picture porn and books such as *American Psycho* (Frankum had a well-thumbed copy) were responsible for triggering Frankum's murderous and suicidal rampage.

Frankum's victims were random, but Manne knows exactly who he is gunning for; all this unhappy sex and violence is the fault of our modern post-religious liberal society which has circulated more nasty sights and sounds than ever before in history and thus created monsters like Wade Frankum as well as making lesser depravees of us all. He says censorship is the answer. Many agree with him.

But wait a minute. What post-religious society? I don't know about Manne's home town, but hereabouts in Frankum's city most folks are baptised, married and buried by their church, swear by its god, and aim to follow its morality. Go along to the Lakemba mosque and see the multitudes, count the number of church schools, which form a major chunk of the education system – look through their press ads for teachers, all of whom must be 'committed to the Christian/Catholic ethos', check out the TV ads put out by the churches (corny old metaphors like pictures of trapeze artistes with a voice-over promising you that deity's wrist-lock will never fail you); spend the weekend cabbing people to the temple, running them to within sight of the synagogue (they slip out and walk the rest of the way for fear of retribution), ferrying severe Scientologists to their office – sorry, church – in Glebe, taking Christians reeking of unscented soap to their various stony pits around town.

And what liberal society? Wade Frankum was a mess of suppressed and confused sexual drives. 'All I'm good for is my arse,' he said when he broke off his engagement to a young woman; but he was still sufficiently homophobic to have to hire a female to do the business for him. And we can be certain of one thing – it wasn't liberals who made him ashamed of his desires.

Manne yearns for the good old days before mass media, when we weren't exposed to all these countless images of blood and fornication. It seems he's forgotten that public torture and executions were commonplace not so long ago; forgotten the biblical, classical and folk tales of Hell and slaughter which filled everyone's heads; forgotten that the horrors of wars, famine, disease and untamed nature were on everybody's doorstep; forgotten that less domestic privacy meant more sexual familiarity. Nothing has changed, only the style. Before, we listened to the Bible story of Judith and Holofernes; today, we watch *Chainsaw Judy* on video.

Manne and his supporters want to censor what they call pornography. They might make a good start by banning the most widely disseminated image of sex and violence there has ever been – that of a naked man being tortured to death on a cross. Developed from the fourth century onwards, and refined in the high Renaissance by masters of the macabre such as Baldung Grein, and by such gifted exponents of sensuality as Raphael, the crucifix has become the badge of institutionalised sadomasochism, the icon par excellence of violent eroticism. And it has become almost unnoticed in its ubiquity: round every neck, on every wall, enshrined in galleries, museums and holy places, dangling from the rearview mirror, hanging in the hall. The church has turned a god into a porno star and created the ultimate pin-up, a still from the snuff movie *Golgotha*; and it has spent the last fifteen hundred years circulating it en masse around the world, with the agency of ruthless dictators, hellfire missionaries, sleazy inquisitors and ingratiating guilt-mongers. And Samuel Marsden, the natural heir to Matthew Hopkins, Torquemada and Cortez, did the appropriate job for the organisation's Australian operation. This is a violent, religious society which encourages its children to fear their reproductive nature and associate it with dirt and pain; thus confused, they are more easily controlled. We could be anywhere in the wide wonderful world of monotheism, where sadomasochistic, homoerotic martyrdom is the highest ideal.

It is not unreasonable to conclude that religious conservatism murdered those people at Strathfield, and that Wade Frankum, a bundle of suppressed confusion and resentment, was its agent. He kept up the fear.

Frankum was an extremist, a rogue. Ordinary mundane domestic violence, under the sign of the cross, is more frequent. Ordinary rape, ordinary gay-bashing, ordinary S&M, bondage and domination is the norm. Ordinary Jesus stretched out in his skimpy loincloth, pinned up, penetrated and bleeding, is the norm. Ordinary mothers hitting their kids, ordinary teachers caning backsides. Ordinary rogues like Frankum. Ordinary myopia like Manne's. An everyday story of Christian life.

I am happy to report that Marsden and his successors did not succeed in entirely subjugating the national spirit. Perhaps Australians retain a healthy collective memory of the very first event which took place upon disembarkation at Sydney Cove, before any of the official business which was to follow. On the evening of February 6, 1788, as a summer rainstorm broke, the convicts came ashore and held a bacchanalian bush party lubricated by gallons of Brazilian liquor (wisely picked up six months earlier in Rio – the only bottle shop in the southern hemisphere), at which they fucked each other silly in the woods that are now the central business district. It was probably a collective hangover-cum-afterglow which delayed the first Christian service on Australian soil. I hope so. I also hope that one day they erect a memorial to this event, too. A pillar of entwining bodies in the style of Gustav Vigeland, perhaps. Ecstatic communions probably took place on this very spot – so let's set the monument right here, next to its more sombre Christian brother.

You don't hear women referred to as 'sheilas' so often these days, though the expression survives here and there amongst the okker and the RSL fraternity. To politer folk it's a bit crude, a bit of an anachronism. But Sheila is more of a throwback than might be imagined. She has quite a history.

She came to Australia as an Irish/Celtic import. Obviously there were a good many female convicts who went by this name, or variations of it. But why should this particular tag be used as the catch-all, and not Mary, or Brigit, for example? There will have been plenty of these amongst the transportees.

The answer may lie in a certain common figure of pre-Christian art which was never completely suppressed by the Christian era. It is even to be found in many British churches, and there is a well-known example at Kilpeck in Herefordshire. It is the image of a smiling woman who squats with her legs apart while her hands grasp and display a voluminous cunt. There are stories of brides being bidden to acknowledge this woman, who gazes down from the corbel where she is carved in stone, on their way into the church (grooms, too, doubtless took notice). This figure is called a Sheela-na-gig.

Many Sheela-na-gigs have suffered erasure or defacement by those who considered them lewd and obscene. More recently they have won back a degree of respectability by being

43

described as 'fertility symbols'. But even this term, beloved of scholars who apply it to any ancient image which is clearly of a sexual nature, may be misleading and euphemistic.

Like many Celtic names, Sheila traces back to the ancient Near East. The Mesopotamian Sheol is an aspect of the great goddess Ishtar – the particular aspect being sexual, as in her regular conjunctions with the god Tammuz. The *nu-gig* was a Sumerian holy woman who served the goddess with sexual rituals. 'Ritual prostitute' (another favourite with scholars) is misleading and tends to grubby up the idea. *Nu-gig* means spotless, pure, undefiled. It is through the sex act that this state is reached and the participants made holy in the sight of the goddess.

So Sheila is an invocation of the great, pure, undefiled Goddess of pre-civilisation, of hunter-gatherers and horti-culturalists, who was duly and gradually destroyed with the coming of agriculture and the entrenchment of the civil project. The semitic Babylonian tells us that eventually the god-king Marduk waged war on Ti'amat, Mother Of All Things, hacked her up and remade the world from the pieces.

She wasn't destroyed completely. She was still around (as Ashtaroth) to irritate the Judaic scribes, and she made it as far as British churches of *circa* 1000 CE. And in modern-day Mesopotamia, the great Goddess is still invoked and associated with momentous events: in 1991 Saddam Hussein predicts that the invasion of UN forces will precipitate 'The Mother Of All Battles'. The biggest, the greatest, is the Mother.

Of that process in the ancient Near East which led to the establishment of Western civilisation, we have since seen a remarkable recapitulation. It has taken place in various countries as a result of the expansion of European powers, and in no place is it more clearly demonstrated than Australia, where hunter-gatherers were rapidly overrun by a people who had arrived for the sole purpose of hard labour in the name of a male monodeity, and who quickly passed from the horticultural to the agricultural to the full-on industrial and the higher reaches of civilised life in less than two centuries. This process has happened so fast that each stage has left copious remnants. The hunter-gatherer population is still present in large numbers, in fact it is growing more visible by the day; and horticulture survives in the people's preference for gardens and suburbs (suburbs are really pre-urbs, pre-civilised). And because many of the first white population were still only part-civilised (when the English called them uncivilised they were being derogatory, but the strict sense was correct), coming from lands at best only recently agriculturalised, these 'Barbarous Fenians', 'Rough, rug-headed kerns' and their ilk used the name of an ancient goddess to invoke a sexually active woman.[1] Baptised by the name or not, she was great indeed (especially in a penal colony) – a Sheila, a Sheela, a Sheol, an Ishtar, a Ti'amat, an Ashtaroth, a Mother Of All Things. Neither Marduk of Babylon nor Marsden of Parramatta could destroy her completely.

But – 'fertility goddess'? 'Fertility rites'? Authorities who use this interpretation of every example of ancient and prehistoric sexual activity will often also claim that the reproductive purpose of sex was discovered relatively late in human history, in Sumerian times in fact; and that this enlightenment led directly to ideas of individual ownership,

---

[1] Neither Brigit, who is a triple goddess of poetry, smithcraft and healing; nor Mary, who is stained with anti-sexual notions of Christianity, would be apt.

families, patriarchies, etc. But if this were so it would make it even less likely that those older images of sex, cunts, priapi, Willendorfs and so on were much to do with 'fertility', since the connection between sex and reproduction would not have been made.

Unless it be a fertility of mind. What is more likely is that in all the millenia of hominid existence up to the coming of the civil ages, sex and its images were not some kind of obvious metaphor for regeneration (there was no plant husbandry), but simply pornographs, advertisements for the sex act. And given this long tradition of coupling for pleasure only,[2] we can suppose that considerable degrees of sophistication were attained, and that these pleasures eventually surpassed the merely hedonistic. Prolonged sexual acts create an altered state – high, enlightened, psychedelic – where the senses are sharpened and expanded; a creative state, a highly charged combination of intellect and intuition. One which, in harness with other activities such as the use of psychoactive plants, enables *homo* to become *sapiens* and invent sophisticated survival techniques, symbologies, cosmologies, languages; and eventually become a very smart culture which knows about animal husbandry, horticulture and birth control, and has found that at best it can live a life of ease, pleasures, contemplations and inquiries without the need to labour hard from dawn to dusk six days a week and to report for reconditioning on the seventh. Not slaving in the fields, nor preoccupied with breeding and raising offspring, they had time for creative (re-creative) pursuits. And sex and drugs (psyche-delics are among other things renowned aphrodisiacs) were

---

[2] Australian Aboriginals call sex 'play'.

tools in the happy pursuit of knowledge.[3]

But this kind of life is incompatible with the promotion of full-on agriculture. The primary civil myth is of Eve partaking of the fruit of knowledge handed to her by old Kundalini, and of the criminalisation of this act by the Boss, who is trying to start up an intensive monoculture on the banks of the Tigris and needs a lot of cheap, intensive labour. From now on sex and knowledge were out, and coupling to be despised, just a necessary evil which pumped up the population, and had the spin-off effect of keeping people feeling guilty and so more susceptible to conditioning.

We are now supposed to be at the beginning of the end of civilisation. We are told that the world is entering the post-industrial age, that leisure is overtaking work in terms of time apportioned to it, that technology has freed us from slavery. Along with this comes the move to the suburbs, the revolution in travel and mobility, the resurgence of psychedelics, the resurgence of feminine power, the break-up of monocultures into pluralisms – all these are signs of the age, and they all echo pre-civilised ways of life. In this post-civilised revolution, the gods and laws established in the Neolithic and Bronze ages as a framework for the development of the agro-industrial system are now anachronisms. When Christians rail against abortion and birth control, for instance, all they are doing is defending civilisation; they are insisting on an ever-increasing labour force just as their predecessors in the Middle East demanded. Since the civil and industrial structures which demanded these breeding orgies are now inappropriate and superannuated,

---

[3] Foucault claims that in Ancient Greece truth and sex were linked in the form of pedagogy, 'by the transmission of precious knowledge from one body to another; sex served as a medium for initiation into learning'. Tutors have been getting it on with students ever since.

millions are born redundant and then conditioned in ways hopelessly out of kilter with contemporary realities. Their educators, popes, politicians, imams, are out of time, straight from Mesopotamia, with their bans on women priests, their six-days-shalt-thou-labour, their vast inner-city temples and their procreative sex. The most hardened of we civilised people (the urban and the urbane) still use condescensions when referring to such things as leisure (lazy); the suburbs (dull, pretentious, ugly); travellers and tourists (grockles, intruders, halfwits); drugs (devilish, depraved); women (problems, harridans, emasculators); birth control (sin); pluralism (chaos, dysfunction) and so forth. And Sheila, having made her long journey across ten thousand years, three continents and seven oceans, first worshipped, later ... bought a few drinks and a box of chocs maybe, given some lacy underwear and a quick servicing – is disappearing, partly due to the objections of those who might have respected her original status. Will we ever see her reclaimed as the endearment she once was?[4]

---

[4] Quite possibly: since writing this I have learned that Dublin dykes recently adopted the Sheela-na-gig as their emblem.

He was a quiet man, shortish, casually dressed. He got into my cab up at the Cross. He was a painter/decorator from Brisbane down here on a job, and he wanted to go shopping for a woman.

It was three in the morning and I'd just started the shift. On the cab radio Zorba was breathily, frustratedly trying to give away a number of cheap local jobs for which — this being Saturday/Sunday — he could find no bidders. As he called for Valium I muted the volume, punched the meter, drove over the underpass and turned onto the William Street ramp.

Miss Birriga — a dark girl, always barefoot in a flouncy black dress; those strong, pale calves — stood and smoked a cigarette in her usual spot at the top of the ramp, looking like a bored hitchhiker. Down on William Street there are a few empty spots. They've either gone home or are off doing business. This first stretch down to Riley is occupied by the glamour dolls in skintight sequins, hot pants, microskirts, enormous hairdos and vertiginous high heels. They stand around chatting, waving, smoking, negotiating, backlit by the car showrooms. A plate-glass tension separates the gleaming motorised phalluses — BMWs, Jags — from the objects of desire. In perfect symbiosis, XJ6 and whore advertise each other.

Across Riley and the girls are less theatrical. They share cigarettes by darkened shopfronts. At the end of William Street we swing left into the backstreets of Darlinghurst, into a dark sodium haze. A cluster of girls in the doorway of a cheap hotel and one squatting at the kerbside, smoking. I slow down for both girls and speed bumps. The girls have simple, wasted faces. Their looks are as slow as their movements. My fare has been silently and keenly observing; now he wants go back up along the north side of William Street, so I disdain a few traffic laws and double back across the eight-lane highway. On this side the sidewalks are wide, in the shadow of hotel and office towers, where a couple of girls are walking together. 'D'you think they're in business?' says the man. It's hard to tell. We cruise on up towards the Cross. Glancing across the road I notice that the dolly blonde who had impressed him has now disappeared. We head up the ramp. The fat woman is on her spot at the corner of McElhone Street: she wears voluminous skirts but leaves her waistcoat unbuttoned to display the glories of her mountainous tits. This is the kind of figure that might have dominated the hypogeum at Malta – that subterranean temple to the earth goddess – and who would be laid out in its circular oratory and there ceaselessly fed and plumped up till she was in a thirty-stone-plus transcendent state and thus inclined to produce prophecies and oracular utterances. Reflecting on this, I fantasise a nightclub called the Hypogeum, a dive where women could go and stuff themselves to their spirits' content, a den of sanctified and guilt-free indulgence. (Six months later in London, England, the prophecy is fulfilled: Planet Big Girl opens.)

Meanwhile my punter wants to sashay down William Street again; we double back over the bridge, but outside the Jag dealership there is no sign of his blonde doll. Down past Riley and left into the backstreets again: here are the same girls, and the same disinterest on the part of my punter. He thinks there may be more women further away on Liverpool Street; I reckon that they're all gay up there. We double back onto William and cruise down to the very end, under the walls of the Australian Museum, where the giant electric sign that is indicating the total square-footage of rainforest left in the world (it reduces before your very eyes) switches abruptly to a twelve-figure sum, increasing before your very eyes, indicating the world's population count. Passing by, oblivious to these dramatic messages, are the two girls he wasn't sure about. I crawl the kerb as he rolls down his window, says g'day and politely enquires as to whether they're looking for a good time, a drink somewhere, a club ... No thanks, they say, they're going home to Balmain. No worries, says my man. I turn around and we head back to the Cross, this time swinging left into the jam-packed 100-yard stretch of Darlinghurst Road, the smell of fried Thai food, the flashing neon, the kerbside hustlers, the pissed punters, the Maori pimps, the cabbies crawling slowly past Bourbon and Beef and the old bright red phallic-shaped pillar box. He sees nothing that takes his fancy so we double back and rerun the William Street route.

We had been cruising around like this for half an hour and I was beginning to get bored. I wanted another fare, a fast easy run over the bridge and up to the northern beaches, or a race down the Southern Cross freeway to Cronulla with fresh air blowing through the cab and the meter turning over quickly. 'Why don't you try the brothels?' I asked him.

'No,' he said. 'It's not the same.'

'What do you mean?' I said.

'It's different,' he said.

He was certainly choosy. Around the circuit we went again. And again. And again. Occasionally he'd ask my opinion of a girl. Most did nothing for me; I gave noncommittal answers. He seemed to be after something slim and blonde. I suggested he try 99 Albion, and the athletics-crazy English girl who expected me to know the names of famous trampoline stars; again he insisted on the street. 'One more time around,' he said, 'and you can take me to North Sydney. My hotel.'

Why should a man prefer the street to the bordel, there being no real price difference? The street means a less mediated encounter, one that begins in the most public of spaces. It allows various pretences about the 'genuineness' of the encounter – neither party may have been looking for the deal until their eyes met: it could just conceivably be a case of mutual attraction. You're then taken to an individual room – it could conceivably be her home – which is far removed from the industrial conditions of the bordel with its power-suited manageress, pistol-packing security guards, closed-circuit screens and cashier's desk, where the business transaction is quite public, and you meet the woman in private; on the street it is the other way round. The Brisbane painter may well be constructing a fantasy, more or less consciously, along the lines of 'I got chatting to this sweet looking sheila, bought her a drink and we ended up at her place. Lovely girl, but I could tell she was a bit hard up so I left a few notes on the mantelpiece where she'd find them later ...' Or he may be chronically shy; or he may get a kick from the idea of exotic pimps lurking in dark corners; or he may be turned on by the idea of a woman independent enough to do without protection. Whatever, this unmediated and less civilised version of commercial sex is flourishing.

So there was one more time around. Then another, then another. The first airport work was coming over the radio; the city was emptying; the calls were from early workers starting out from the suburbs; and here I was tediously donkeying up and down William Street, a slave to this man's patient desire. He was clearly well suited to his trade, where such dogged assiduity is part of the work and where watching paint dry is an interesting and necessary task.

In all this time the only women he had spoken to were those two beneath the ever-increasing world population figure, but now as we cruised once more up William Street there appeared on the kerb a slim blonde in a tight black catsuit, posing vivaciously, hands on knees, smiling brightly. 'Pull over,' says my man.

The woman's beaming face was at the window. It was strong, confident, direct; it had fine lines of age traced over its features. She was beautiful; she gave me a hard-on.

'Whadderyer prahces?' said my man gruffly.

'Massage and sex, half an hour, thirty dollars.'

He ummed and ahhed. She was right for him. All the looks he wanted plus the motherly touch: 'I'll take care of you, sweetheart. You need loving. I'm very, very good. You don't have to worry. My room's just around the corner.' He stared at his hands. She reached in and tickled him under the chin, soothed him, cajoled him. 'Whadderyer think?' he said to me. I told him to go for it (*go* being the operative word). 'Yeah, I think so,' he said. He pressed forty dollars into my hand and climbed out. She took his hand and they turned away and walked down the side street. I saw him suddenly loosen up as he went, and then put his arm around her as their pace quickened.

I read Patrick White's *Voss* at Bellevue Hill where for a couple of months we rented the ground floor of a duplex. Most of the time it was intensely hot. The jacarandas were in full bloom and the bamboo shoots on the back lawn were sprouting up at two inches a day. Kookaburras had stolen the fish from the little pond. (Unlike some, I never felt these birds were laughing at me. The bird which did seem to have some mysterious piss-taking point to make was a white cockatoo who hung upside down from the telegraph wire across the street and made attention-seeking noises as I passed by: an Australian tarot card, a local version of The Hanged Man.)

I read most of the book in the small bedroom with its old plaster mouldings, floors paper-rotten with white ant, billowing net curtains, ornately wrought iron bars arabesquing their way across the windows; a faint mildew in the air, and a brilliant white light slicing in at an angle from outside: the leaves of a tall palm, the glowing red pantiles of the neighbouring house, its wall of orange pebbledash, the tall clapboard fence and the hissing of the lawn spray all day and through the night. Weeks of bleach-bright heat alternated with binges of sluicing rains. Constant news of flood, fire and assorted catastrophes in a threatening ring around metropolitan Sydney, which itself remains unscathed and inviolate.

voss on bellevue hill

Voss takes a trip from Sydney to the outback, to the wild unknown, in the 1840s. Radiating unbearable weaknesses, the manic German and his handful of followers trek off after the great dark heart like Freud in search of the id. They begin to putrefy long before they die. Ill-equipped for a journey to such an altered state, they pay the price. But Voss is redeemed before his sticky end by telepathic communication with an allegory of Wisdom in the form of a dark, rebellious young woman. This woman lives in the house of a draper at Potts Point, and she is the niece of its rich respectable owner, who is one of the expedition's patrons. By the time she hears the conclusive details of Voss's death, which have taken years to trickle through, this woman has become a successful headmistress. In a last valediction she declares the explorer to be a brave man and a great spirit.

Here on Bellevue Road, Brigit was struggling through a mental bush, involved in battle with an ugly and savage demon which was attempting to destroy her. When I remember that bedroom I see the black-and-grey covered paperback copy of *Voss*, the stained-oak dressing table with its mirrors and potted lily, and I hear her voice justifying a suicide she felt was imminent. It seemed to her the only way of destroying that demon who was torturing her with contempt and derision every hour of the day and which appeared invincible but for its dependence on her life for its own.

For hours through the night in the sweating bedroom Brigit howls and spits and wails, and mourns and murmurs and repines. She frightens me. She is fearsome. I am through encountering her with logic, it only seems to lead to a grave. I imagine her dead – the body, the tiresome practicalities, the misery of dealing with her family – then feel the horror of her loss, and I begin to wail. I sob this despair out to her. After a while she seems to react. I think good, this is working. I am distraught but I am also beside myself, watching, considering. Something is changing in Brigit. I remember that when you mimic an infant's crying it will tend to stop, confused, curious. Brigit stops. She is shocked. I subside. She declares that she will not kill herself, but only so as not to distress others. 'Ever dutiful,' she observes with a numbed irony.

We're still in the double bind. Come this far and she's still not granted the most fundamental of autonomies. I have helped persuade her – for the moment – to renounce her right of choice over her own life or death. What right had I? I had no right at all. This is dog-eat-dog. I'm fighting my corner.

One day while Brigit was out her father called from England. He has the voice of a respectable Australian professional – it resembles that of a long-time weather forecaster on Sydney TV, grey and furry. But not unagitated. He was aware that Brigit was in a desperate state. As he spoke he appeared to take on the character of the Potts Point draper who when confronted by his niece's 'mental fever' sends for the rich and established Doctor Kilwinning, whose state-of-the-art psychiatry consists of bleeding the girl with leeches. Maurice urged me to urge Brigit to take drugs. I'm all for drugs – unrestricted access to the compleat pharmacopoeia – but it's a question of which may be appropriate. He was recommending lithium. After a brief trashing of every development in postwar psychiatry and psychology he declared his conviction that 'depression' was in the genes: his wife had exactly the same condition, and had attempted suicide at the same age; and regular fixes of lithium from then till now had saved her life.

Man, I thought, lithium's a dunce-out; turned your wife into your kind of woman, has it?

Lithium is one of those surface drugs. They circle around you but they don't address your being. They tape you loosely to the secure-yet-flimsy rituals of the world, the skin on a cup of cocoa. They don't go into the middle and they censor any news from the red heart. With lithium, you have enough problems as it is dealing with its effects of dysfunctional memory, reduced concentration, slowed thinking, confusion, disorientation, difficulty walking, slurred speech, blurred vision, ringing in the ears, nausea, vomiting, headache, muscular aches, twitches and tremors, weakness, lethargy and dry-mouthed thirst.

But is Margaret really your kind of woman? The first time we met your first words to me were a serious aside, an apology for your wife, who was skipping around excitedly like a pigeon-toed schoolgirl. I'd 'have to excuse her'. Perhaps she'd either overcome or not taken her pills that day.

What was this drug, a rite of passage? Brigit's turn now, right age, right lineage, twenties and tormented, and as far away from home as you can get on this earth ... just like her mother.

The only thing to be thankful for is that this is one thing that runs in families that is not genetic. I suspect a domestic virus with a human face.

On the cover, Sidney Nolan has made Voss's face resemble Freud's. Both of them came to nasty ends: Voss of exhaustion and decapitation, S.F. of a cancer that destroyed his face and made him stink so badly that his dog wouldn't go near him. Both men were terrified yet flirtatious of the forces that would destroy them – the id, the desert. In both of these expeditions neither leader will acknowledge any higher human authority, and in both cases the deistic authority available is paranoid in nature and therefore not up to the tasks demanded of it.

Voss and Freud – but Central Europe does not have a monopoly on this style of pessimism.

AUSTRALIAVILLE

*

I had heard Maurice's ring despite my earplugs, which I removed (yellow circles of foam tipped with orange wax) and replaced after our conversation (I had been politely non-committal about his wishes). I wore these earplugs day and night, and seldom removed my sunglasses. I was writing about music, usually in the airy, bright front room, and I was insulated from the rush of traffic on Bellevue Road and the glare of a white melamime desktop. The pale cream ring-dial telephone sat on a carpet of heavy whipcord which was a peaceful fading maroon colour – of blood flowing at the appropriate rate.

All this – the weather, the house, our preoccupations – lent a certain knife-edge to the atmosphere. This was compounded by the clinical surroundings up here on the hill. The astringency of grapefruit and lemon trees; the clean, million-dollar houses; the Mercedes; the security patrol cars; the streets quiet and pedestrian-free, avenued with fat, knarled evergreens. Saturday mornings were the only time pedestrians appeared: men in black, women sombre, boys with tasselled cloths poking out from their trouser belts, girls in knee-socks and velvet and patent-leather shoes. Keeping alive – just – this idea of walking.[1]

Brigit has already travelled over a good deal of this country. Scuba-dived in the Whitsundays, hitchhiked through western Queensland and to Uluru, read *The Female Eunuch* on the train

---

[1] 'And your horse; I must send the man round.'
'I came on foot,' replied the German, who was now caught.
'From Sydney!' she said.
'It is four kilometres, at most, and perhaps one quarter.'
'But monotonous.'

Voss

to Adelaide. She was even a convict – a month's community service for a driving offence at Cronulla. She has been considering surface drugs – coastal drugs if you like – and has been paying visits to a psychiatrist at the mental health centre in Bondi who is recommending them. A short course of tranx, maybe, or tricyclic or neuroleptic (he's not specific) – 'Just to keep you level while you get yourself sorted out.' She is inclined to give it a try, but then again, she knows her mother.

'There's plenty of land along the coast,' says a young man who abandons Voss's expedition and turns back with a couple of others. (They don't last long.)

In one sense the failure of Voss's project (perhaps too of Leichhardt, upon whom the story is based) is a failure of hierarchy. There is a rigid class-system to the small band: the autocratic Saxon Voss; the frail English naturalist; then the immigrants – a brooding and confused poet, a drunk, an ex-convict of the working classes, and a simple-but-strong boy. And an Aboriginal guide whose status is entirely Other. What hopes has a journey like this when its leader remains so thoroughly aloof as to be autistic?

Brigit knows her mother, who knows her own place in the class of things: firmly and declaredly subordinate to husband, God and Jesus. (Fostered by a priest at Bourke; some say sexually abused by the man, some might see no evil; she has not been sufficiently interrogated.) Lithium has become as integral to her as communion.

Ethnobiologist Terence McKenna would classify lithium and its ilk as a 'dominator drug', one which reinforces these hierarchies, a toxic clampdown on an individual's autonomy and imagination. These drugs are distinguished from 'partnership drugs', psychoactive plant hallucinogens from cannabis to opium to peyote to psilocybin, in use since pre-civilised days, and significantly responsible for the development of modern *Hom. sap.*'s extraordinary cranial capacity and intelligence contained therein – and thus our capacity to survive. These drugs make your eyes sharp. McKenna goes on to float the notion that 'Pure democracy is thoroughly psychedelic.'[2]

There was no practical reason why Voss and his band should not have survived in the wilderness, but all except the ex-con Judd were overburdened with civilised attitudes. They could not conceive of going native, going pre-civilised in order to survive. They would not adapt. Psychedelia was unthinkable.

The tribes survived there fine. Psychedelically certainly, democratically ... maybe. What whites who support land rights and other protests are seeing in Aboriginal people, among other things, is the attraction of shamanism. The shaman is a powerful healer, herbalist, ecologist. Through these contacts pre-civilised values get assimilated (travel, walking, is another) and form part of a post-civilised world that is trying to be born. It may make it.

Bellevue Hill is residential but has no neighbourhood. There are one or two scattered shops, mostly with fawning proprietors. Two friendly bottle shops within walking distance ... but no caff, and what's a neighbourhood without a caff? No restaurants, no pub. The nearest neighbourhoods are around the suburb's fringes at Double Bay, Rose Bay, Bondi. You could say Bellevue Hill is a dark heart, quiet broken only by flocks of parrots; nothing else but trees, and vast, endless expanses of civilisation. And those black humans with their ritual walk.

---

[2] *Food of the Gods* (Bantam, New York 1992). McKenna is particularly concerned with a 'revival of the archaic attitude toward community, substance use, and nature.'

There are one or two scruffier houses like this one. There is a comfortable rotting three-piece suite on the front porch; the mynas are nesting up there in the fuse box cupboard. From here at night a shrub gives up a heavy scent of vanilla and you can look way down there to the downtown highrises and to their right, glowing like green kryptonite, the Harbour Bridge, the city's Uluru.

Some afternoons Phil, who lives at Rose Bay, drops into the interior, comes by with some grass and delivers us from the twin tyrannies of short-term memory and late civilisation. We sit around the spaghetti bolognese. Brigit tells Phil that she's decided against the doctor's drugs.

'He was all right after a while, he didn't pressurise me. He was listening very hard.' Then she recalls, 'The first time I went in there I was, you know, just looking for one good reason not to top myself, then and there. And you know what, the place was deserted! I couldn't believe it. I finally found someone who said everyone was off in a room at the far end of the place watching the Melbourne Cup. So I went along and watched a horse race.'

'It's the Aussie approach to therapy,' says Phil.

It was after this that Brigit began to buy lottery tickets.

'Civilisation is hooped together, brought
Under a rule, under the semblance of peace
By manifold illusion'

'Supernatural Songs', W.B. Yeats

Every morning Major Foveaux heaves himself out of the ground at the corner of Bourke and Fitzroy. Flourishing his whip he marches down the switchbacked hill, followed by three lanes of impatient vehicles, calling this thoroughfare into being.

(Many of the Ancients carry whips. They had their Christ, and they had their thieves, and they had their own provincial punishment park.)

Foveaux calls out the patch of grassy ground at Crown Street: it springs into life. He names the Touch of Class bordello at Riley: it materialises as if out of a mist, its balconies of intricate ironwork hung with tropical vines, half-hidden behind banana palms. He moves on, calling out, waving to the left and right, and to the bare earth as a carpet of tarmac unrolls before his boots; and above his head, where a canopy of plane trees is suddenly synthesised from the elements. As is the Victorian pub, the Bauhaus garage, the warehouses and rag-trade outlets, the parking meters and discarded takeaway meals, and drunken tribespeople – punk, Aboriginal – stupe-fied in doorways.

The roads around Calvary must have looked like this, Foveaux tells himself with pride. Then he reaches Elizabeth Street, and turns to face his children: a heat-haze of traffic that is backed up over the hill, fingers drumming impatiently on

63

doors and wheels, the odd honk.

'I am Foveaux,' he declares, and his statement crackles over every car's radio; and with a magisterial gesture he strikes the ground in front of him with his whip, where a manhole materialises. Foveaux climbs down and pulls back the cover. The traffic surges forward. Another day can begin.

All over town the Ancients are going back in, their names and their territory having been established for another turn of the earth.

Well-known British travel writer Jan Morris is in town, publicising her new book on Sydney – this is her second book about the metropolis, of which she says she's extremely fond. Generally speaking the reviews have been reservedly polite. On an arts TV spot, her interviewer has a query: why is there no mention of Mardi Gras? After all, it figures significantly in the city's life.

Morris's reply is brusquely polite: as far as the Gay and Lesbian Mardi Gras is concerned, this huge street festival, Australia's biggest and now in its fifteenth year, which every March draws tens of thousands to it and culminates in a massive parade through the city and an all-night bash at the Showground – she's never heard of it. Pause for the sound of gobs being heavily smacked.

You couldn't chide the woman for choosing not to cover Mardi Gras. She has a right to her own angle on things. But it's too bad that someone in her line of business, presenting a social and historic overview of the town, should be unaware of one of her subject's major annual events – and declare the fact so complacently. It's like studying Ganymede and not noticing Zeus.

Her interviewer might have gone on to point out Jan Morris's personal connection with sexual unorthodoxy – as everyone knows, she was James Morris once upon a time. But this was a polite show, in a set full of soft furnishings in dusty pinks and pale blues. And an assertive feminine show, since the host was a softly greying, tweedy man who came across like some kindly old Sapphic from Lady Margaret Hall, and the guest was someone who had been dedicated enough to cut her way through to femalehood with surgical knives.[1] Perhaps this act was Jan Morris cutting her way through from paradoxy to orthodoxy. To a position where news of the weird and wonderful might never again reach her.

In a way I don't blame her. Orthodoxy must have seemed secure. Sexual deviations were not looked so kindly upon in the days when Jan was a man, long before Mardi Gras in Sydney was even putative. And in the early years of the festival there was a good deal more aggro about, undiminished at that time by the thought of tourist dollars[2] or the protective presence of the Dykes On Bikes.

But it's a fine word, Deviation. And my experience of Mardi Gras prompts the question: who are the real deviants in this affair? Where does the real imbalance lie? With the festival-goers in all their celebratory joys and bizarrities, or with the celebrated fundamentalist Fred Nile praying for rain so that the whole affair might be ruined, or with the drab, morose, so-called normal folk I sometimes chanced to ferry home from the straight nitespots of the Cross during that night? For these latter people, the prefix *hetero* is a misnomer. The men in particular are no more adept at accommodating the women in

---

[1] The ritual mutilation of adolescent Aboriginal males by slitting open the base of the penis is said to be done in honour and imitation of the vulva. This treatment also makes the penis wider at the base and thus much more of a fun object for women. Who is running this show?

[2] The New South Wales Tourist Board still refuses to publicise Mardi Gras.

their lives than they are comfortable with the female part of their psyche. Their relations with women are based on the politics of neolithic hierarchies and the confrontations of business, sport and other war games. They are afraid of both sexes. Their sexuality is actually *homo* in the sense that it is self-contained; communication is stunted; they are monosexuals, autosexuals, *timeo*sexuals. (While their women are victims, hangers-on, else struggling to dump this whole carry-on.) For true heterogeneity you have to go to the gay community; ditto for generous expression, for a balance of logical and lateral processes, for a psyche where the female can have something like a decent status. Gays are the true heterosexuals of this world.

For queers and their allies sexual expression is an all-or-nothing business, whereas the straight person's affairs always seem to remain half-expressed: propelled forth by political licence and personal desire, yet held back, cloaked, desensitised. For six months I took gays and straights home from their nocturnal entertainments, and to put it simply: at the end of the night gays are happy and straights are not. The difference was never as stark as on Mardi Gras night.[3]

Around four in the morning the bash at the Showground is just beginning to wind down. Parties which are miniature carnivals in themselves climb into my cab in a mêlée of sequins, stockings, white leather cowboy chaps, bare behinds, musky scents, marijuana smoke and racy banter; more often than not we end up at some other party – at a warehouse in Mascot or a terrace in Surry Hills. These are known as recovery parties.

---

[3] Life is not so sweet for gays elsewhere in Australia. In the state of Tasmania for example, despite a five-year, high-profile campaign, sex between consenting adult males is a crime which carries a twenty-one-year prison sentence.

AUSTRALIAVILLE

Long after daybreak I find myself taking people to the stage-three parties at which they recover from the first two: the motormouths, acid trippers, young English girls cadging my fags for their joints, people going to the beach, or else entirely satiated now and nodding off into intermittent comas on the way home to Darlinghurst or Elizabeth Bay. And then, groups of dour men coming away from King's Cross: Been to Mardi Gras? – Ah, no mate, I mean, each to his own and that ... got nothing against them like, but ... what was it like? They're groggy on beer and whisky and there's no sparkle in their tired eyes. They talk about the club they've just come from: What about that lesbian double act, eh? I could have really fucked the dark one, got a hard-on right away ...

Dream on, guys, but you're missing out on something. They seemed to know it, in a grudging kind of way. Ah yeah well, maybe next year ... I dropped them home, stupefied in soggy leather jackets and badly-fitting jeans, to go dream on their mediated versions of exotic sensuality, the hot lesbian double acts and the rest. As for the real thing – maybe next year if sufficient courage can be screwed up. And as they grunt and snore and visions come in fits of not-so-rapid eye movement, their carnival-going compatriots, senses still sharp from creative drugs and elative company, are partying on.

Earlier, TV presenter Sophie Lee had been working her butt off amidst the floats and pzazz, struggling to keep pace with procession, crew and script. Lee, a Nordic type in her mid-twenties, slim as a chance, is fronting a new show for prime-time TV called *Sex With Sophie Lee*. It's a grab-bag of vox pops, professional talking heads and telecine of red-light districts. It aims to be light-hearted and educative and open, but slinky red dress or not Ms Lee presents things like a nervous young schoolteacher, propped up on her stool tight-faced and smiling only with her mouth. At best the show is remedial – but this is all that can be said of even the best TV. And the old compulsion remains, the felt obligation to counter each light note with some warning about 'responsibility'. Enjoy, says Sophie, hardly managing a smile, but let's not forget love: love is holding hands amongst the apple blossoms; whereas lust only happens in red-light districts – says the camera's shorthand – and there's not much in between. Watching monotheist TV promoting sex is like seeing Dr Goebbels attempt to endorse Judaism. Come on in! *Sex macht frei!* Oh really?

The day I'll enjoy one of these programmes is the day one gets me horny. There's certainly much more useful and entertaining instruction in many a porn video or magazine. The day shows like Sophie Lee's give us stiff cocks and people fucking everywhichway will be a good one for heterodoxy. The day sex isn't reduced to two large knockers, a red light and a condom; and love isn't some blossom-tinged godfearing state-sanctioned reproductive unit or some such deluded notion of stability, is the day I might take such PR seriously. Till then I'll carry on counting the variety of ingenious items they find on which to unroll a johnny in place of the real live member for Loinsville, the immortal, invisible, companionless god, the cock of ages whose unseen hands conduct this charade. Till then the lovers' discourse will probably remain, in Barthes's words, 'in extreme solitude', 'ignored', 'disparaged', 'exiled from all gregarity'. 'The distinctive mark of modern souls,' says Nietzsche, 'is not lying but *innocence*, incarnate in lying moralism. To have to rediscover this *innocence* everywhere – this may be the most revolting task a psychologist today has to perform.'[4]

---

[4] *On the Genealogy of Morals.*

AUSTRALIAVILLE

The innocence of *Sex With Sophie Lee*; the innocence of dour straights dribbling away from the Cross like Jesus's blood; of cabbies who have avoided Mardi Gras for fear of 'picking up more than just passengers'. The innocence of the national rugby league side, indignant at being goosed by their British opponents (the Brits are not afraid to demonstrate via affectionate bum-squeezing that this game is a disguised orgy). The innocence of the Queen, goosed by Paul Keating. The innocence of women queuing up for the Anglican priesthood. The innocence of soft-furnished TV studios. And the innocence of Jan Morris, emphatically Not Guilty of Mardi Gras.

(Mitchell Highway song)

They used to tell us the names and addresses of the people, and what plane they were coming on, and we used to have to follow them up. All nationalities they were, English, Greek, Ceylonese. The Brisbane Good Neighbours Council, that's what we called it. And we used to have to go along there and ask if they've got any problems and sort them out and that sort of thing.

I needed that exposure because I'd grown up in the outback; but unlike some out there I was up with the news and I used to listen to *Voice of America* of a night-time on me shortwave radio, and at four o'clock ABC news programmes and all that. So I was up with everything in the world, probably more than the city people. I was out near Longreach, halfway out to Alice Springs. My grandparents accompanied the surveyors that took the line through to Longreach in the 1880s when telegraphy came in. And to get to a dance you travelled 110 miles (and 110 miles home), and when I got there, there were probably only two white girls and I had to look at them and then more or less begin to dance with them. So I might have only two dances all night, drove 110 miles each way. In those days the cars weren't as fast as today; there was no laws related to drink and drive, which meant a lot of people got really drunk. It wasn't a crime, it was expected of you to drink and drive in those days out in the outback. But there's no comparison these days with fast cars

71

and that. See, those line-straight roads, they used to go to sleep while they were driving and everything in those days.

It was that hot in the summertime, we used to have a whippet. It'd be that hot we'd be staying in hotels out there, we had nowhere to stay. We used to put the whippet window, place it horizontal and get it going as fast as possible to get the breeze on our face it was that hot. And in regard to cricket and that, we used to play cricket, football and that. I don't drink, but in those days I used to drink quite a bit, and me mates were drinking, and half of us became alcoholic. Those outback places look all right, but they got nothing to do, and a lot of them they go into town and drink, and the grog's pretty strong, so if you keep drinking like they drink, they drink from four in the afternoon to midnight, and on Friday from four in the afternoon till Sunday morning. Right through. And Broken Hill's that sort of town – in the old days they used to fight at the drop of a hat. But they've been through hard times, those people. I mean I can understand their mentality, I'm not saying I agree with it, but that's how they live, and they're trying to hop on the tourist bandwagon now, because there's not much there, is there, really. They got a lot of historical stuff. You need to listen to their story, and you need to tell your story. They need exposure to you, and you need exposure to them.

Where are we now? Cobar?

Well, they came out of the ten-pound fare and they'd be out here a week and they'd say 'Ah, can't stand the bloody flies,' and this started the whole thing going, they'd go back. And they'd be back there six months, and they'd change their mind and they'd give another ten pound to the Australian government and that means they got their fare paid out and they did it three or four times. And of course the Aussies got a bit sick of this, and it should have died, it should really have died, but you get *talking*, like, this is the first trip I've had a chance to talk to the Japanese, and I haven't had a lot to do with the Japanese people and I find them lovely people! I couldn't believe it. What had I heard? Well, I hadn't been told anything, it was just that I hadn't communicated with them because I hadn't had the opportunity. We had war with Japan, of course; if you go up to Darwin, if you go in the underground tunnels there you'll see the whole – all that took place between the Japanese and the Aussies. And that created a friction image. But because they're very well educated now, the Japanese people, most of them can speak enough English to get by, whereas the Australians are not educated and they can't speak to Japanese people. So this trip, I went around and I made it me business to spend time with Japanese, because I know they could talk my language, but I couldn't talk theirs. So I said I'm going to give them time, I'm coming across from Perth, you get in the dining car, you know, for two days with them. Yeah, I did all the centre and up the Northern Territory to Darwin and Kakadu. And I did Kunanurra, Broome and Dampier and all those places. Even for day trips I used to travel 400 kilometres just every day on a bus to go to a day out.

I went in June, and we'll get home in August sometime. Got a son getting married. Got eight kids, eight lovely kids. We didn't count them, we were out west, and when you think of the children, it didn't matter what class, colour or creed you were, when they're out in some of these outback towns they all have big families, irrespective of class, colour or creed. The Aboriginals had big families, everyone had big families because they all seemed to have at least eight or nine, yeah. For a start, in the cities you had big house rents and that. Do you know what – my mother gave the house away to a poor couple of teenagers when she left the town, for four thousand dollars! And the darn thing was worth about fifty thousand! You know, on the coast it would be worth about a hundred and fifty thousand, but out there – so the couple came up and they said, 'You leaving us?' You know she was getting ready to die, sort of thing, seventy, ah, eighty-odd she was, and she thought she'd come down and live with us on the coast, and we had all this – you know, those four bedposts, and the marble-top tables, and all sooty oak and all that? Everyone of the neighbours came in and she'd say 'You can have the table,' or 'You can have the . . .' – old days, the 1880s dishwasher, how they used to wash the baby in the big bowl? – And she went around giving all that sort of stuff. We didn't care. Out in the middle of nowhere, and when she bought the house in the 1930s she said she only paid five hundred pounds and everyone had a go at her because it was the dearest house in town. Five hundred pounds. But she said she'd never sell it and she couldn't take it with her. So she gave it to this young couple who came on they were broke, and she was pregnant, the girl. She said to them, 'How much can you afford?' And they said 'We can go to four thousand dollars but we can only pay ten dollars a week. We can't give you any interest. So that means it's four hundred weeks we can pay you, ten dollars a week.' This was not too long ago. Anyway, that's how they work out there; there's a different lifestyle and you got to understand the mentality.

But I knock around a lot and I sense loneliness, there's a lot of loneliness in the world. A lot of the people they were lonely and I sort of introduced the English to the English and the Irish to the Irish and the Scots to the Scots, then I'd try to put on barbecues and things to mix them all up, you know, so they can get exposure t'others, and that way, I told them if they last for six months they wouldn't want to go home. If you can stand it for six months your mentality changes, you're just as bad as the Aussies then! You don't notice any difference! So anyway that's the way I taught them. Some of them came out here and they used to wake up of a morning and they'd say, 'What are we doing in this strange place?' So a lot them did go back in the early stages. And a lot of them that did go back are sorry they've gone back but they can't get back into the country now because it's tightened up.

We called ourselves the Lucky Country for years, we had no problems. We were really too laid back and we'd got it all easy. Although you'll see a lot of struggles about – you know those lines all through here, they were hand built with shovels and they used to die and all that. And you know those Aboriginals, they were elderly people and they used to just die. When you read the history, the beautiful history of this place ... but it's a real big struggle. But we seem to need England to, you know, give another picture of life and to widen our horizons. You know, we got no history here. We got this sort of history that you're hearing about in these pockets, but we haven't got the Bucking-ham Palaces. But still, if Britain didn't have royalty, and I'm not knocking royalty, but the point is, you've got your wedding of Di and Charles and all that, and if people went over there it's a tourist thing, you know? Broken Hill's got those storytellers and that; it's a tourist thing, it brings money in, and Britain must have got a lot of dollars through people going from Australia and all these countries to there, and the first thing they do, they go and have a look at Bucking-ham Palace, you know. I don't know why. But that's a part of their culture and their history. Yeah.

Australia's current problems. Well, we had it easy for too many years, as long as I can remember. I'm actually fifty-eight and I'm retired, I retired and I got a major payment, salary-related, right? And I invested it and it was earning more than I earned when I went to work. Because I've got kids in year 12 and 10 going to college, I got a mate down the road from our place, he's into real estate and he likes me to come down and help him. Well, in the six months I work for him I can earn more dough than I earned from the government in twelve months. So I go and I work for about six months at half-a-day at a time, and then I've earned enough for twelve months, and I don't touch me Super, which is earning more than I was earning before at work, so I'm in a sitting position, aren't I?

But I'm fifty-eight and I've worked, I've been all over the state; I know that state backwards, I know every town backwards by name, and I used to know the people by name. And for instance if someone said, 'Tell me about say, Rock-hampton to Winton,' I'd say 'Rockhampton, Gracemere, Duaringa, Bluff, Blackwater, Comet, Emerald, Anakie, Bogan-tungan, Alpha, Jericho, Barcaldine, Ilfracombe, Longreach, Morella, Winton.'

Now, I had relatives in Katoomba, my second cousin I think it was, and he owned the Town Centre Motel. He doesn't own it now, he sold out. What he used to do, he put in a manager eleven months of the year, and for the other month he used to look after it, my second cousin. We lost track of this mob, and then we found 'em through a set of circumstances, and he used to invite me down – but he used to go travelling Australia for eleven months of the year, and for the one month of the year, he used to go back to Katoomba and look after this motel and let his manager go away. So he just sold it not long ago, and I think he's – I don't know, I'll ring him from Sydney. I'm not getting off because I'd like to go through to Canberra, we got a wedding next week, so I want to go through to Canberra and I got to get home by the sixth to measure the suits. The wedding's on the eighth; it's me son's, so we don't have to prepare. But we used to go down to this guy, he used to have, in Katoomba, he used to invite all them relatives up from all over the state, and he'd have a weekend there. And he was into history and they'd do all these personal trees and all that, and anyway, he did this, and we used to go to it, you know, to meet them all. And he used to do the trip that I sort of did this time, you know, he'd go up there and he'd spend a month in Darwin and probably a month in Perth and all these things and just go around and take his time.

Overseas? I've been going around here all the time and I haven't seen it all yet. I've been to Tasmania and those places, but she doesn't like going overseas. I might be going to Rio – someone talked me into going to Rio! Yeah, for the carnival. I don't know whether it's any good. I've got to talk her into going yet, she said to go on me own, and I might.

My grandparents accompanied the surveyors that took the line halfway out to Alice Springs, and the only thing I can tell you – my auntie was the world's youngest morse code operator at the age of seven, and that must have been back in the late 1890s, '99 or something, because there was an American boy out there, and they had the line, the telegraph line, the morse code, and they put her on it. She was seven, he was nine, the American boy, and they communicated, it was headlines in the paper. She was the daughter of this postmaster in an outback town, and their houses in those days were pretty small and they had the morse code near to the bed and it used to tap away; well, she grew up with it, and then when she learned the ABC she put it all together just straight, like that.

Now the only other historic thing about ourselves is: my grandpeople were *Kennedys*, yeah, and when we had a look at the certificate it showed Kennedy, Wexford. Now, when I was eighteen Mum said to me, one day it came up on the radio there was a young Kennedy in America elected to the United States Senate – J.F. She said to me, she said, 'This guy who got elected today to the United States Senate', she said, 'he might be a relative of yours.' And I said, 'Why, Mum?' And she said, 'Well, look where he comes from.' And she showed us her mother's birth certificate and that, and they were Kennedys, her father's, from

77

Wexford in Ireland. Then, as he came into the Senate some family photos came out and he was – at eighteen he was as thin as a whipstick. At eighteen I was as thin as a whipstick; and she used to carry them around in a little purse, the both of us, and some of the mates couldn't even pick which one. But we changed a lot after that. Hell of a lot. But that was – when? Eighteen – that's forty years ago. I did get a shock when he was shot, but I don't get attached to anyone in high places. And I don't sort of think what could have been or what would have been, and I don't try and trace things like that, you know. It's nice to know all these things, but the things you find out about your ancestors are unreal – I found out a couple of things recently which shocked me. Yeah, these people from Katoomba, this really shocked me, so I wouldn't talk about it with anyone else other than you because you're going away and I'll never see you again. Well, the thing that I found out they done was something that I've always detested. It was my pet hate, you know? Anyway, what happened is they – these people in Katoomba – they were pretty rich, and they used to ply around all the towns where everyone was buried, and they found out where all their past was. And they flew to Ireland, and they went and interviewed people, they were tremendous, you know, they had a lot of money, this mob. And they went and interviewed, and they run into grandmothers or someone that knew someone and that – and what really shocked me, one of – I don't know how it came about, I haven't had a good talk to them, but they did tell me last time, that there was a case of incest. And it really knocked me over, you know, it really knocked me over.

You might say it's quite common. Well, it surprised me because I came from out west and I suppose there were a lot of male chauvinists and things like that, you know, where these shearers – you heard that bloke at Broken Hill, how he talked rough – but they're not underneath, they're – I see through

78

these people, it's only an incident. When you hear people talking like that, it's a mask, though, and I just smile and say 'You bloody bugger', you know, that sort of thing. Well, where I come from, if there was anything mentioned of homosexuality, they'd kill 'em. They'd bloody kill 'em! You either had to be a total one hundred per cent man or – no, not even ninety-eight – that's the type of mentality they were. I grew up near the Tree of Knowledge. The Tree of Knowledge is in the town of Barcaldine. I saw hundreds of shearers fighting in the main street using palings out of fences. 'You rate 'n' I'll rate you', you know how this bloke was talking yesterday? Well, Broken Hill's got a lot of history behind it, a hell of a lot of history, they been through all sorts of troubles. The Australian labour movement was formed at a town called Barcaldine, they'd fight at the drop of a hat. They either loved you or they hated you. There's no greys. And to me that's sad, because they would even – and as I said, if you weren't one hundred per cent man you weren't – I've seen detectives meet trains and even in the early days before long hair came in, if they'd got off the train with long hair, the 'tives would get them and say, 'Get back on the train, you're not getting off here. We've got no' – sorry, they'd be policemen – 'We've got no CID branch here and we're not looking after you and we're not going to be responsible for your safety.' That's how tough I've seen the town. And as I said I've seen shearers fighting in the street.

One day I witnessed, after a big fight in the street, new-and-old-age shearers, I witnessed them going to hospital, one bloke got put in hospital. And the diehards were that sour on this bloke, they went into the hospital next morning and took him out of the hospital, and he had broken legs and arms and everything, and belted him again because – ah, terrible, the things I've seen. You know, that's really bad, you know, the mentality of the past, you know how you read history, the

79

things that went on? And they thought absolutely they were doing right. It's just like all over the world. Some people can't bend. You need to be flexible no matter what you believe in. A lot of these people have been through that much trauma and that, the only way they survive is to fight. But that's not the way. All the psychologists tell you, you discuss things, then you come to a compromise, you know? And to accept one another for what they are, not to change them to what you want them to be. So that's why I like hanging around with them because, I mean, I never met a person in life I didn't like. I've never met a person in life, and I say that sincerely, that – they've done a lot of things I didn't agree with, but as far as I'm concerned I have never met a person I didn't like. And I've been around all over, so as I say, I didn't agree with a lot of things they did but that didn't stop me from liking them. Because I knew underneath that mask they'd have a lot of good there and I could learn from that good. I've met some people, completely diabolical – and I've seen more Christianity in some of those than I've seen in some of the churchgoers. You see, it's a theory thing with them, isn't it? It's a lot of words up in the top area and you can get into argument and intellectual stuff all day long and you'd go off your rocker. But the real thing is whether your neighbour's dying of malnutrition or not and whether you're helping him, that's the real issue.

I went through all sorts of stages in my life till I got to where I am now. When I was eighteen I thought I was right, and when I was twenty-eight I thought how stupid I was when I was eighteen. And when I was thirty-eight I couldn't believe where I had been, you know? I couldn't believe it. And the things I used to believe! And this was a result of exposure to other people and more understanding.

What's the name of this movie? Is it any good?

Home Alone.

After Christmas the Bellevue Road house was sold, so we stacked a ute with furniture and trundled over the Harbour Bridge. I had taken my earplugs out in time to hear Anna Nassauer say 'Ah, yer North Shore people now, you won't be coming to see us again.' Inference of Sydney's haute bourgeoisie holed up in their hillside palaces in recently reclaimed bush (Cromer Heights, Terrey Hills, Ingleside) amongst the media stars and rich wide boys, close by the big glamorous stretches of beach; Narrabeen, Dee Why, Newport. Business in North Sydney (power dressers and postmod officescapes), parents growing old in Cremorne (urban Surrey), taupe linen jackets from the boutiques of Mosman (Golders Green): why pay the bridge toll to slum it on the south side?

Turn right at the end of the bridge and you're in Kirribilli. The technical North Shore at least. The waters of Port Jackson lap against its piers, low cliffs and tiny beaches where tiny crabs scuttle around crash-diving into the sand at your approach.

If a neighbourhood has a reasonable quantity of old Toyotas and Honda Civics, and a smattering of seventies Kingswoods (Dukes-of-Hazzard style six-cylinder Fords) immaculately kept else customised to the widewheeled teeth, and a couple of young women in black chiffon skirts and Docs, hair dyed blue-black like two prodigal members of the Addams Family and walking hand-in-hand – then you know there's a little bit of imagination left in amongst places like the Federal Reserve Bank, the

81

Governor-General's official residence, and the yacht club. Here be also a number of flaking hostels and other lowly forms of accommodation; and the petty crime rate (as reported by the neighbourhood watch newsletter) is reassuringly active – front door jemmied, VCR ripped off, etc – in this peninsula half a mile square bounded by the harbour and the bridge approach freeway. Its name means Good Fishing Spot and its shore is always populated with people hanging lines from the rocks or squatting on a milk crate on any of the several ferryboat wharves. Part of Kirribilli Avenue, which fronts the harbour, is sheer rockface, fifty foot high and curtained by vines, glistening with water-courses which dribble down to the roadway where an explosive bush of full-blooming Busy Lizzie spills out across the sidewalk. Up above is a flaking colonial manse, and next to it a cluster of sixties apartment blocks. If you walk on, the roar from the bridge diminishes to near-zero and evergreens and gums arch above you. Parrots feeding in flocks on the tops of banana palms ... smaller redbrick deco apartment blocks ... garbage stacks spilling onto the pavement ... and here's the stretch of nature strip where that Alsatian lays its cables. We've come to reside at the top of a decaying three-storey block perched high above the roadway. We stand on the steep steps and study the view: the opera house head-on across the water, a cacophonic cluster of pricked ears. We are practically downtown, a fruit-bat's flight across the harbour (they flock across at night from their hangout in the botanical gardens).

It's the hottest time of year and here at 'Quay View' everybody's windows are open and everybody's business flies out, bounces back off the neighbouring side wall and lands in everybody else's business. There's an American who is always talking loudly to an unheard companion about his business deals; a nervous solo parent who constantly squeals away at her giant fourteen-year-old son for some misdemeanour (he's built like a Hereford and tends to knock down her china vases and soil her carpet); a young pommy who holds late-night gatherings at which he holds forth endlessly in a disgruntled, home-counties, minor-public-school accent on the theme of why-should-I-have-to-support-welfare-scroungers (he means dole bludgers) with-my-taxes.

The roaches, like the crime rate, are at a reasonable level and hustling around like pantomime Fagins. The shower curtain is a polythene map of the world. Brigit found this place. It's cheap, and the views around and about are enough to cool out the most hardened of claustrophobes. The harbour waters are strangely odourless (no seaweed), but the floating quays, rocking in the swell, smell refreshingly of rotting fish and diesel oil. It's a change from Bellevue Hill and the static of the ultra-civilised, and the empty pond.

I share a birthday with Angela Brazil (1868–1947), the prolific writer of girls' school stories. This discovery led me to read some of her work, and a story I shall never forget is *The Luck of the School*, which was written *circa* 1920, and whose scenario is a ladies' academy-by-the-sea in the aftermath of the Great War for Civilisation, as it called itself at the time. The flowers of the English gentry having been cut down on the fields of Belgium, arrogant nouveaux riches are buying up the old estates, and one of these now owns the land on which stands 'The Grove'. What's more he's common, rude, and is closing down traditional rights of way across parts of his spread. '"Most suburban! Shows he's only accustomed to live on the outskirts of a town," scoffed Brenda scornfully.') But the nasty arriviste's real crime is this: he's nicked the girls' maypole. And if the girls don't get to dance around the maypole this spring the consequences will be dire, for the maypole is the 'Luck of the School'.

Thus Angela's heroines, who are nothing if not assertive and intrepid, find themselves in a battle to regain their pre-civilised rite of phallic worship in the face of its suppression by an insensitive, urbanised tyrant. Led by Peggy Hunter,[1] they even attempt to steal the twenty-foot-long fetish back from beneath the very walls of their enemy's mansion, such is their passion for the pole they call their mascot. But before they can manage this, Brazil's gorgeous Amazons find themselves having to rescue the landlord's daughter when she nearly drowns while bathing in the cove. After this they can of course name their terms, and as the maypole is re-erected on the site of its age-old glories, at a spot significantly named Robin Hood's Green – another chunk of rural myth surfacing here in intimations of the Wild Green Man and his virgin bride. It is duly bedecked and celebrated come the day. The rescued girl is made Queen of the May, and falls in love with Peggy Hunter. The new squire becomes more respectful, and the girls regain their land rights. Paganism has triumphed.

Brazil also has a character called Lesbia in another story, *Loyal To The School*. Some consider A.B.'s stuff is all unintended, subliminal. If so, it makes her bosom buddies with Sybilla de Bondorf, the Angela Brazil of medieval European painting (*see below*).

Meanwhile I'm taking the train home from work, which trundles into Milson's Point station around half-three on these occasions. I stand in the vestibule as the double-decker, smoked-glass and airconditioned carriage jerks to a halt. Then like heavy theatre curtains the doors slide open to reveal – O spirit of Angela Brazil! – a hundred excited schoolgirls in Marian-blue smocks, frozen for a split second in a chaotic

---

[1] A double-barrelled surname would be even more apt: Peggy Hunter-Gatherer?

chorus line before they crowd eagerly towards me. If I don't take care I shall be trampled in the stampede and be carried, flattened, all the way to Hornsby. It would almost be worth it. But I negotiate my way off the train, along the platform and through the booking hall, still engulfed by a rushing ocean of girls in blue. Down the main drag of Kirribilli, into the backstreets, the tide doesn't let up, and outside the sweets 'n' smokes shop there is a brief mountaineering exercise as I traverse piles of blue backsacks dumped on the sidewalk.

Looking at these girls in their strangely backdated uniform, what strikes me most are the differences between individuals: fat, thin, Nordic, Levantine; skin texture, hair, shape of lip, body language, pigeon-toes or wide strides; every girl's idiosyncracies insist themselves and seem doubly real, vividly set off by the powerful statement of her blue tabard. Curiously, this phenomenon appears to contradict the fundamental idea of regulation uniform, which is to conceal the individual behind the mask of the organisation – you're in the army now, and all that jive. But here each girl's beauteous glow, whether lost in thought or animatedly rapping, tenor or soprano, renders the underpinning of her appearance – the uniform – quite invisible. When I see these kids on other occasions, bedecked in secular drag, stuff that's flogged to us so we can express the essential *me* – strange thing: they are just a bunch of people dressed in whatever's current on the street, they are subsumed by what are essentially soft billboards, clothes which are either pushing other products like Coke or INXS, other ideas like Save the Whale or Republic of Australia, or, more commonly, are ads for themselves. Decal'd and logo'd, the trainer and the jean, the sweatshirt with COUNTRY ROAD writ large across the chest, the backpack whose pocket flap is one big label saying BILLABONG, are at once product and advertisement. (You'd think they'd pay you to wear them, but this principle goes out the window when a sandwichboard is made of cotton or leather.) The soft billboards set up a static-like buzz of a neon sign or the fluorescence of a TV, through which it is difficult to notice or examine the creatures who provide the scaffolding. That baseball cap says BOY but it may be a false clue ... The individual is concealed. Walking down crowded George Street or through Paddington or Maroubra, there's nobody in sight: I see only moving clothes, animated commercials for the rag trade. This is disappearance à la mode. By contrast, these girls in Kirribilli are stark and clear: their uniform has stripped them completely naked.

As well as the fish in the harbour, Kirribilli has Sydney's best fish shop, wet or fried. And as well as the convent school it boasts an ancient Jesuit academy with a statue of St Aloysius in sixteenth-century knee-pants standing in a corner of the junior yard. In fact – peace be unto them – the place is swimming with Catholics.

It is the fish that attracts them. The cool, chaste fish, badge of the first Christians. The creature whom the early Fathers strove to emulate by virtue of its reproductive strategy: sex without contact. The creature stocked in convent ponds, around which nuns walk and pray, 'For he is chaste as they.'[2]

The fish is also held to be oracular. Notwithstanding the famous flounder of old Europe, Jeshua – Jesus – means fish. This is why the first Christians associated chastity with visions. These men's bizarre notions of continence functioned as a neat apologia for the contempt for women that they shared with much of the antique world, and supplied them with a perfect

---

[2] Robert Graves, 'A conversation at Paphos, 43 AD', in *The White Goddess*.

excuse for avoiding sexual contact: celibacy at worst would bring you closer to God, and at best would make you a prophet, they claimed.[3]

Because its generative method makes it more plant than animal, the fish will have been endeared of men such as Tatian and the Syrian Encratites of the second century CE, who would not eat meat and were celibate because they claimed to abhor any behaviour which mirrored that of a beast, because a beast, (in the form of the tantric serpent) was held responsible for the 'fall of man'. But reproducing like a plant, the fish is a special beast. Is it this plant-nature that supplies its wisdom? Perhaps some of the wackier of the early Fathers, the desert mystics and their like, either anti-drug or out of drugs (or out of their minds on drugs) calculated that the effects of psychoactive plants could be attained merely by mimicking their 'celibacy'. The odd thing is that they called this 'continence'. Watching clouds of pollen shaken from a male plant, wafting across on the breeze and subsequently becoming entrapped and ingested by the sticky vulva of the female flower oozing with visionary resin, 'continence' is the last word which springs to mind. But one can imagine early Christian man in a terrible quandary: struggling to eradicate pre-civilised methods of transcendence, struggling to be sober and yet desperately seeking visions, he concludes in his panic that an act of mimicry which is the crudest of analogues will cause him to come face to face with the Big Picture. (Did he dream of his nocturnal emissions floating off on the wind to meet and mingle mid-air with a similarly projected egg from some distant labial launchpad?)

The problem is that the technique just doesn't work. It's

---

[3] A Catholic fish-Friday is another communion, but more blatantly cannibalistic since one gets to actually slice up, chew and swallow on the flesh of Jeshua.

topsy-turvy science. Ask any tantrika. The only visions obtained by sexual abstinence are ones of sexual sustenance.[4] But rather than abandon the method, the furthest-out of these learned men were deranged enough to hope that at least they'd get some hint of a heavenly buzz if they were to cut off their own seedbags and toss them to the breeze. The first-century Alexandrian teacher Origen is notorious for doing this, supposedly following his lord's teaching that those who make themselves eunuchs for the kingdom of heaven are blessed. Castrations are not that popular these days, but the preoccupations of early Christianity have lingered, to say the least. The contemporary calls for continence hide extraordinary longings and confusions and desires no better than the pinafore dress disguises a schoolgirl's individuality – the priest's robes have always been transparent.

It is hard to imagine that these schoolgirls from the Sacred Heart convent might form a loving attachment to a maypole. The luck of their school is a more stylised version of phallic worship which parades every spring: the cross, with its more prosaic representation of rising flesh in the figure of Jesus. On this figure itself many painters have been inclined to depict a tumescence beneath the loincloth: Van Heemskirck's *Man of Sorrows* is a fine example of this, and of an intensive eroticisation of images of Jesus' suffering which took place throughout the Renaissance. There is an extraordinary and subliminal painting by the nun Sybilla de Bondorf – *St Francis Kneeling at Prayer*[5] – which depicts the saint at the crucifixion, and which

---

[4] See Origen, *De Principiis*; Porphyry, *On Abstinence*; Methodius, *Off Sex*; Eusebius, *On No Fun*; etc.
[5] Reproduced (for other reasons) in Greer, *The Obstacle Race* (Secker & Warburg, London, 1979).

is rife with signs of sexual excitement in all five characters present including the donkey. But it would take a Rosicrucian to go as far as bedecking the cross with flowers, and I know of no Christians who would dance around the object and then elect a sex goddess for it. Feminine and sexual resurgence comes from other quarters these days.

But Angela Brazil's feminist *The Luck of the School* was truly of its time. After the War for Civilisation, which was vividly lost by all participants, women were suddenly everywhere and doing everything: getting suffrage, flying planes, writing books, family planning, on the turn, on the town, sniffing coke, smoking dope and dancing their butts off. They had the field to themselves since the competition was lying under fields elsewhere. Thus did a brief flash of post-civilisation emerge. The West was wild, feminine, surrealist, psychedelic and multisexual, from Hollywood to New York and all the other towns listed below Alfred Dunhill's monogram. There was a great party going on. And accordingly in *The Luck of the School*, the girls' reaction to years of carnage was not to erect an emblem for the dead and mourn at its foot like women below the cross, but instead to resurrect a pole and party with it. Their pre-civilised gesture is a sign of the times. Civilisation soon reacted to all this by spawning the real decadence, a plethora of Duce's and Emperors who once they had bred enough young men again would screw things up nicely for another few decades. Now today also women are threatened with backlash. The lesson could be, hang on to your maypoles and observe two things which at first may give off a whiff of paradox: first, capering around a giant cock can be liberating – in Angela Brazil it leads to a Sapphic affair; and second, doing this in uniform is the way to express the real you.

'The degree of a nation's civilisation is marked by its disregard for the necessities of existence.'
Our Betters, W. Somerset Maugham

Everything in the Journalists Club is smeared with nicotine. Nowhere more so than the library, whose panelled walls, glass-fronted shelves, portraits-in-oils of past secretaries in dark gilt frames, cabinets and padded chairs all glow in rich tobacco-coloured hues.

Virginia King sits at the head of the long, brown, glass-topped table. She's running a fiction-writing seminar. Virginia King is an active anti-smoker. Throughout this evening session the heavy cut-glass ashtrays remain unravaged and glittering, by her order.

The bar is an umber fog, humid with beer and spirits and flashing with slot machines, into which we eventually tumble to consume our various drugs – paracetamol, port wine, cigarettes.

Outside, in the sodium-lit night, is a line of cabs along Chalmers Street: a red glow and wisp of smoke at every wheel, and on their roofs are illuminated ads for Peter Jackson, Benson & Hedges and Winfield 35s. Beyond, the clocktower of Central Station stands tall and slim, and glows like a Virginia King.

I feel bestial in the last hours of darkness. Wide awake (strung out from mountain to ocean, wide as this city), I need a waking dream.

Coluzzi's opens up at five in the morning to a rush of cyclists in full touring/racing drag, fluorescent harlequins with wiry calves and rattling flat heels jabbering away in full-volume Italiano. Where do these guys go to work to be up so early? Melbourne? They don't stay very long, some just come in to fill up flasks. It's the cabbies who sit around talking shop and swapping jokes. One particular old-timer always holds court in this tiny bar: he's like some dry music-hall comic in his white flat cap, weathered red nose, cream-coloured seersucker suit and white slip-ons. He tells long stories about priests fucking nuns, bus drivers or each other, else pontificates on the day's race meetings in his soft abrasive voice, cracked lips hardly parting except to draw on his cigarette or pull from a glass of *caffè latte*, while everyone laughs and the crockery clatters and the espresso machine roars.

Joe Coluzzi makes the best coffee I've ever tasted, rich and smooth and nutty. If it wasn't the best I wouldn't be sitting here tolerating all the raucous camaraderie. He's a jolly old fellow, hard and sinewy. He was a champion boxer in the fifties and around these walls there's many a picture to prove it: fighting poses, journalists' caricatures and signed portraits of the great entertainers – *To the Champ with fondest regards, Frankie*, or Tony, or Dino. Sometimes, since Joe is always strutting about spouting snatches of tunes, they ask for a song and he punches out variations of the soulful, tearjerking, I-love-you-Mama genre – really badly. To a boxer, a song is an opponent.

This maudlin sentiment towards mothers – where does it come from? Why these tearful, abject, syrupy ingratiations? It's guilt which stirs the churn. Men who get silly about their mothers are of an age by which time they have laid so much shite up the mothers of this world that the pangs are beginning to bite. Or perhaps their wives aren't giving them enough tit (and have run back, black-eyed and beaten, to their own mothers) and so they hunger for the good old days of mama's mammaries. Whatever, it sounds atrocious. But the cabbies love it and Joe likes to please, just as he likes to know everybody by name and have our orders off and running as soon as we step in the door. Joe Coluzzi is happily servile.

There are other pictures on the wall too, ads for little theatre shows and art exhibitions, and even at this hour, a harbinger: a serious, balding young man wearing round glasses, sat on his own in a brown tweed suit earnestly studying the *Sydney Morning Herald*. Once breakfast is over and the cyclists and cabbies are gone Coluzzi's will stop being a transport café and turn into an artyfarterie, its little mushroom stools spilling across the sidewalk beneath the bums of the sensitive.

I got tired of the noise in Coluzzi's, tired of the boxing fans who produced conversation as subtle as traffic lights, and tired of Coluzzi's seven-foot-high beefburger son who always calls you 'Champ'. So I started having breakfast on the other side of the King's Cross underpass at the Bar Hernandez. Across the underpass, across the Med. From boxing to bullfights. From the Coluzzeum and slaves in combat to the Plaza de Toros and a ballet between a beast and a suit of lights.

AUSTRALIAVILLE

Hernandez never closes. You step inside its old brown bay window at 5.30 and it's almost empty. Then you register a Beethoven piano concerto playing on the big stereo, oil paintings hung around the walls – portraits of dark, thoughtful women, a bullfight ... and there's 5207 in the corner studying a book; I always took him for a thoughtful type, in his understated casuals and his immaculate white stationwagon.

Hernandez's coffee isn't quite as good as Coluzzi's but he does a world-beating lemon Madeira-and-poppyseed cake. Around sun-up there's maybe five or six customers, reading, writing, listening carefully to a big romantic symphony or some flamenco exposition, or striking up a philosophical debate which becomes open to all. I sit in the window and watch the sun rise, look out across the grass embankment and ornamental trees and see ravers straggling home across the footbridge. And more often than not some dark dishevelled darling with smudged mascara and long bare legs which disappear into a glittering little black dress will ask me to take her home from Hernandez to Rose Bay or Moore Park (the empty roads, the dazzling mass of backlit plane trees on Ocean Street, the rush of cool air); and coming after hours of raucous darkness, this presence next to me of a limpid, glimmering creature completely satiated by a long night is a perfect reawakening. And *she* pays *you*. You the beast, fast being tamed; she in her dress of lights.

When Brigit comes home from belly-dancing class, for example: she usually brings a friend or two, and they spend the rest of the night laughing, drinking, and shimmying about the flat, jewellery flashing, hips swaying, bongos racing, Brigit's hair blazing like Uluru at sunset.

At other times she is withdrawn, and has such a frail sense of her own worth. Examples: a subliminal voice tells her she's useless, 'a piece of shit'. She is constantly expecting to be attacked from the periphery of her vision. She will be paralysed for a day, 'feeling like an imposter in this world', empty, yet full of unspecific angers. She panics and abreacts, curled up and quivering, crying for her mummy. She has a strong sexual appetite, but feels inexplicably frightened of the business, especially at night. (When she does let go, with plenty of wardrobe, make-up and props, she's got enough power to light up all of Kirribilli, and demands a reciprocal force.)

This is a good fishing spot. Every time we dip the line we reel in another piece of history from the bottom of the harbour: another long-held fear finally voiced, another incident from a childhood of chronic abuse. A father who roared and flailed; a silently suffering mother, ravaged by anti-depressants; above all, normal, respectable Christian parents, upstanding members of the neighbourhood watch, home-owners, professionals; like so many whose daughters want to be fucked until it hurts because that's the only way they get to feel anything (you know the song: 'Harder, HARDER ... FUCK ME YOU BASTARD ...').

There has been no sexual revolution, only sexual publicity. Behaviours remain essentially the same. Erotics and violence were chained together since the expulsion from the garden, and from the first time you were hit for playing with yourself.

'The lot of the women prisoners must surely have been greater than [that of] the male convicts ... several have not recovered yet from their treatment at the hands of the Major.'

'To be remembered by all there was his love for watching women in their agony while receiving punishments on the triangle ... it was usual for him to remit a part of the sentence on condition that they would expose their nakedness, it being considered part of the punishment. And the poor wretches were only too glad to save their flesh and pain.'

Two fond remembrances of Joseph Foveaux, quoted by Hughes in *The Fatal Shore*. And Major Foveaux was a run-of-the-mill father of the nation.

Histories of the convict years – a huge chunk of white Australia's history – give the clear impression of a nation whose youth was spend under the whip. Can we talk of a country which has suffered childhood abuse? Born in chains ... in constant fear of pocket fascists and rapine clergymen ... dragged through Gallipoli like some prep school initiation torture ... hating itself (Menzies and the repugnance he felt whenever arriving back in Australia) ... unassertive when sober ... unsure of its identity ... deferring (the 'cultural cringe') ...

White Australia begins to resemble black America. Pommy fans taunt Aussies at the SCG with a chorus of 'Union Jack on the Aussie flag/Doo dah, doo dah'.

And a defensiveness. On arriving, I heard: 'So you've come over here to take jobs from our kind?' And on leaving, I heard: 'Australia not good enough for you then?'

Sometimes Brigit despairs: 'I'm not cut out to be an artist. I think I'm special but I'm not. I just want to go somewhere and be *normal*.' Nationally, this translates into a desire for conventional living in a self-effacing module in a standard neighbourhood. It's a way of hiding which is less painful than remembering. Ninety per cent of residential Australia is pure suburb, swathe upon swathe of it: these topographies conspire to erase history.[1]

But Australia can boogie just like Brigit. They party hard here. It's the primal formula of sex-with-violence further abstracted to pleasure-with-aggression. A party is known as a *rage*. 'Maintain the rage,' said Whitlam, shortly after the Queen's Governor-General had removed him from office. This seems to have been taken as an instruction to party on.

It's a question of ferocious fun. All-nighters turn into endurance tests. The inner harbour echoes to the cannon fire of pyrotechnic displays almost every summer night, and Kirribilli is shrouded in a thick pall of barbecue smoke as countless varieties of music and conversation waft into my window from all directions. By day sidewalks are dwarfed by the aftermath: mountains of garbage, 90 per cent of it empty bottles, and the Pacific Waste truck, low on its springs, crawls through the streets like a hung-over cockroach.

Is there a clue in that post-disembarkation rage of February

---

[1] Together they drifted to a forgetful Adelaide suburb.' (Chatwin)

AUSTRALIAVILLE

1788? Was this extended Dionysiac orgy a vigorous attempt to delay the morrow's inevitable arrival of Sisyphus?

Public entertainers maintain the pleasure-with-aggression principle. Clive James, ruthless as Magwitch, *punch* lines a speciality: Germaine Greer's comedy of polemics; the sour glamour of Barry Humphries; the manic Brett Whitely, his work decorative and angry; Patrick White, sweetly relishing bitter herbs; and Yothu Yindi – sensuous dances and demands for land. The polemic, the sarcastic, the dark, the satiric, the demanding. Enjoyment comes literally with a vengeance. (The fuck-me-harder routine can turn into a weapon which results in damage to the fucker – exhaustion, bruised pubic bone, etc.) Once-abused children, people in their twenties with the ghosts of childhood still on their backs, begin to identify and understand the source of that abuse and thereby empower themselves. In this way Brigit becomes an allegory of Australia as she uncovers more and more past humiliations, teasing out information not only from her own censorious psyche but from her parents, who are reluctant to talk for fear of shame, pain and loss of status. She must try and get closer to them than has ever previously been allowed. In the same way, the Australian Prime Minister has just put his arm around the Queen, a status-levelling event which caused horror in traditional quarters: How dare you touch Mummy like that! What are you, some sort of nasty Oedipus?[2]

The country is looking at its past with a clearer eye. More

---

[2] But the damage was done. It was early '92, and from that moment on Ma'am's status was never the same. The sordid secrets of her family would leak steadily out and eat through the respectable façade like battery acid. The chickens would come home to roost and lay their shit on her doorstep like a bill from the taxman. We lived a few doors along from the colonial splendours of Admiralty House and would watch the

and more Australian histories – academic, fictional, cinematic – are appearing. The 'convict stain' has all but disappeared (people now desire and pretend to convict ancestry) and is being replaced by another kind of guilt – remorse for white man's degradation of Aboriginals (sometimes this is constructive, sometimes merely mawkish, viz. Mr Hawke's tearful performances). A new confidence and assertiveness means that complete political independence is now imminent; just as it is certain that Brigit will eventually become a republic. You can tell by the way they dance.

---

old royal Rolls emerge and see the Queen sitting alone in the back like a little girl inside a big black coffin. She looks discomforted. Is there a voice in her ear singing *Hey little bird, fly away home. Your house is on fire, your children are alone*? Her 'annus horribilis', when she would see both her castle and her credibility go up in smoke, is just beginning.

William Redfern was a young naval surgeon tried for supporting a mutiny and transported to Australia in 1801. He got a free pardon a couple of years later, and is famous for cleaning up conditions aboard the convict ships. He's known as the father of Australian medicine, and it is said that public health in the colony began with Redfern: working with convicts and administrators alike, he had the largest and most popular practice of the times.

The suburb they named after him lies to the immediate south of the city centre, and is a typical slice of run-down inner city. A whore whom I regularly dropped off at five in the morning at her terraced house in Pitt Street would always get me to wait and watch for her safety until she was indoors, even though the neighbourhood appeared deserted and it was no more than ten feet from cab door to front door. Geoff Beardmore tells student cabbies that Redfern has recently become known for its rag-trade outlets – 'But when the sun goes down, so do the shutters. You don't window shop in Redfern.' It's M13 country: knife attacks on drivers, bricks thrown at passing cabs.

Redfern is known even abroad as Sydney's Aboriginal quarter, but you don't meet many 'pure' Aboriginals here; there's been plenty of racial mixing – most have only a hint of the typical heavy-browed and square-jawed skull, and their skin is often nearer white than black. Like the coloureds, the whites here tend to be students, musicians, men under pressure, undernourished children and overworked mothers. I took an old white gent home once, to his council block on Walker Street: all the way from Bondi he seemed to take relish in complaining of his diabetes and his respiratory diseases, enjoying his cigarette as he did so.

Recently the Redfern police let a TV documentary team follow them around for a while. These police were either foolish enough to forget they were on camera, else sufficiently naïve to believe that the world at large would not bat an eyelid when it saw on its prime-time screens this force's routine abuse of Redfern's people. The most notorious example was of a policeman's party, at which one officer blacked up his face and posed, grinning, with a noose around his neck in a callous parody of recent Aboriginal deaths-in-custody. The affair caused an uproar, but not as many sackings as were clearly due.

Young women I picked up early mornings in Redfern would almost invariably be heading for one of the methadone clinics in Surry Hills or Darlinghurst, else a hospital further afield. There was a thin, blonde white girl dressed in black who told me she was a prostitute, and three months pregnant. She brought into the cab the strong scent of warm, sweet milk: it was as if she had just been immersed in a vat of it. The father of her child had run off three months back, but they were about to be reunited, and with their baby planned a new life out in the western suburbs. I dropped her at the Camperdown hospital where she was going for a touch of the pre-natals. I wished her good luck with her life. 'Yeah, thanks,' she said, looking at her belly, 'I only hope it's not born with withdrawal symptoms.'

Redfern has its own small hospital, the Rachel Forster. One of my regular riders was one of its doctors, a quiet middle-aged woman who lived in an expensive new high-rise block at Circular Quay. Her journey to work always involved a long detour to Woollahra in order to pick up a cake from a fancy pâtisserie there. It was I who would fetch the cake from these sweet-smelling premises before driving over to Pitt Street in a haze of marzipan. I would drop her off, make sure my windows were closed so as to retain the pastry's intoxicating aroma, then take a run along the main drag which was populated by baby buggies, drunks, rich young women looking for fashion bargains at Country Road; but most of all, queues: of nervous-looking types by bank cash dispensers; of tired-looking people at bus stops; of irritated-looking people waiting outside the Social Security offices while semi-trailers belching black exhaust thunder by on their way to Port Botany.

Here's a health to William Redfern, wherever his shade may reside. I'll always associate his name with comforting smells and wearisome sights.

It was fear that drove Brigit to the Twombleys. The fear that if she didn't go, they would come and seek her out and witness her fragile state. She felt more vulnerable on her home patch. She declared this trepidation, without any degree of jest, after Marcia Twombley tracked her down on the telephone. Brigit's father, playing long-distance social secretary, had given her the number.

'I hate it when he does this,' Brigit said, 'I've told him often enough but he never listens.'

Marcia is a cousin of her father. Brigit has never met this branch of her family. All she knows is that Marcia is a schoolteacher, her husband an engineer, and they have two children in their early twenties. 'Come over for dinner one Sunday,' says Marcia, 'and you can swim in our pool.'

So we took the train to Turramurra, passing in transit such disorientating and interstitial station signs as Wollstonecraft (I was back in St Pancras churchyard at the squat cube of Mary Shelley's mother's tomb, and then racing over the arctic ice in search of Frankenstein's beast); and St Leonards (I was playing in the sandpit of a Hastings guest house in 1947. The house was a gloomy place, overhung by evergreens. A toy skeleton dangled from the bathroom ceiling, and there was an equally skeletal giant of an old man who was a residential guest and who wore baggy suits and had extraordinary piercing eyes and who terrified yet fascinated me. It was this gentleman, known as Aleister, who taught me the semaphore of the dinner plate: cutlery at right angles – not finished; cutlery parked parallel – finished. Mr Aleister was soon finished himself. He died during our stay, and there were some very peculiar people coming and going. I later learned that I had been tutored by the Beast himself, the bizarre genius Crowley.)

The afternoon was overcast. Young Richard Twombley picked us up at the Station and drove us the short distance to Epping, through a beige-grey landscape of wide, empty roads and long ranks of large low-roofed houses shrouded by pines and gums and palms. They could have been American houses except that they lacked basketball net, flag and satellite dish. On the way Richard told us he was a physics graduate and was now studying at an evangelical Christian seminary. At the Twombleys' big bungalow we met Marcia and Eric who are both greying, quiet and conservatively dressed in shades of brown. Susan is a blonde in blue jeans and white sneakers. Richard was dressed ordinarily enough – check sportsjacket, viyella shirt, knitted tie; but his long black beard and John Lennon specs on a prominent nose stood out somewhat and gave him the appearance of an orthodox Jew.

They welcomed us with white wine in the kitchen. Item number one was genealogical bonding. We gazed at a wall collaged with photographs of the family. Who was who? Which uncle was which? And so on. Soon the heavy pattern of likenesses woven along blood lines and across consanguinitic branches formed a generalised blur until all these figures and faces had become one single generic person viewed as if through a fly's eye or kaleidoscope; seen as if in a full-length mirror, this being emphasised by the long rectangular frame which held five generations of pictures: sepias, oblong studio shots, tiny black-and-whites from the forties and fifties, garish contemporary wide-screen colours. Stand and behold the many-headed beast thou art, thy repeated lips and angled brows, thine hundred eyes and ancient gaze.

My host leads me down a panelled hallway hung with ancient frames ... 'And this is my great-great-great-great grandfather the first Earl of Inbredeen ...'

'Really? And this?'

My host is suddenly uncomfortable. A cloud darkens his countenance. He twiddles his fingers.

'Hmm – ah, there's the gong for dinner. Shall we ...?'

But further pressed at table about the medieval portrait of a startlingly attractive young woman with the strangely contemporary hairstyle and make-up, the young heir reveals that 'We don't like to talk about the Lady Caroline.' However, it eventually transpires that a certain madness is supposed to run through the female line. And then all conversation suddenly dies as the scarlet-clad figure of a beautiful, petulant young female appears below the gothic arch of a distant doorway ... v/o: Clarissa! From the instant I set eyes on her I was captivated ...

I slipped out of Hammer Horror[1] mode as we adjourned to the living room for dinner. Susan's boyfriend had arrived, a soberly dressed and deferential young man who when asking for the mint sauce or salt addressed his hosts as 'Mrs Twombley' or 'Mr Twombley'. Prompted by Brigit, Richard soon became

---

[1] What might be the enduring appeal of the gothick? This signature image: this rotting castle and its corrupt landlord, its Bluebeard, de Sade, de Rais, Nosferatu. Terror induced by these protagonists is balanced by the comforting evidence that their house is falling about them. We see a

very genial and talkative and went on at length about astrophysics in a manner not likely to make him a great populariser of the subject. No point either in asking him how one reconciles this stuff with fundamental Christianity. I've met these snakes before. God is simply a singularity; theology a matter of politics and morality; inquiry is limited to exegesis of St Paul's tangled thickets of circular logic. Heard it all before, and though the boy's coy smile seemed to be inviting me to take him up on it I wouldn't give him the pleasure of demonstrating that a monotheist can worm his way out of any impasse, any of the million contradictions thrown up by twice a thousand years of history, with the alacrity of a rat up a drainpipe fuelled by a faith which, far from passing all human understanding, is inspired by animal, Pavlovian terror.

What version of such terrors might have been inspired in this boy by these modest-looking progenitors who now sat opposite him? A fear of the unknown perhaps. Young Richard follows science as far as it has currently gone, is invited to make further researches – and baulks at the prospect of the ineffable, the singularity. It's too terrifying, and the only way to deal with it is to worship it. Or has he discovered himself to be underequipped intellectually to crack the higher codes and, rather than admit this, preferred to declare them unbreakable, holy, unapproachable?

'You must never, *ever* enter this room . . .'

What was the secret of that forbidden domain? What horrors lurked in the depths of Castle Inbredeen, and

---

simple analogy of civilisation in its dying throes, a dangerous, bloodthirsty and pathetic criminal within, and we must beware. In vampire stories particularly we are watching the subversion, literally and figuratively, of blood relationships.

what might Clarissa already know of them? She threw back a glass of wine with insouciance and leaned slovenly back in her chair, a defiant smirk on her vampish young face, challenging, daring anyone to reprimand her for such a disrespectful attitude. But no one spoke. The seventh Earl glanced at her nervously from time to time. She had been sent to try them ...

Richard held court. His family was quiet and acted like guests. Had he been sent to embarrass them? They had unwittingly spawned a junior patriarch of great assurance and a degree of scholarship, whose hairy face and glinting lenses could not have been more contrasting to the light complexions and modest composure of the rest of his kin. His ancient, Hasidic presence dominated the table like a revenge, some ancient guilt returned to haunt them. Backlash with black beard. But Richard's image betrayed a fundamental frailty when he told me how he liked science fiction and exalted an indifferent passage from a much-read and dry-papered novel of Ursula LeGuin. This scene was painted in insufficiently lurid colour and conjured up a half-hearted mushroom-gothic of minarets and pointy arches, and it was peopled with rival Viking-like spacemen battling it out with arcane threats and finalistic statements. A drab apocalypse indeed. But it seemed like heaven to Boy Blackbeard. He went through the passage explaining why I should be impressed. He would have had a better chance of convincing me that the Holy Trinity was democratically elected.

After dinner we all went down to the basement. Here were revealed the cultural underpinnings of the establishment in the form of shelves lined with old books – fifties Penguins, Graham Greenes (two copies of *Brighton Rock*), Kingsley Amis and the like. The den's centrepiece was an old player piano, freshly varnished, a glossy brown monster which was fed with samples of the Twombley's copious library of pianola rolls. Marcia slotted in a copy of 'Keep The Home Fires Burning', and as invisible fingers banged out the march in tones harsh and bright as an outback sun she sung along in her enthusiastic soprano as the words wound by on the roll's autocue. This was followed by 'There'll Be Bluebirds Over the White Cliffs of Dover', which was delivered with even more relish while the rest of us supplied back-up vocals, and I wondered about the ornithology of the cliffs of Gallipoli.

Richard by now had departed, away to some religious rite. We below were in the throes of a ritual equally arcane and atavistic. Susan took her seat at the pianola, switched it to manual and opened out a copy of Lloyd Webber's 'I Don't Know How To Love Him'.

'I don't know how to love Him ...' she sang, and with her hands she rivalled the pianola's invisible ones for expression. Her voice was genuinely despairing, as if she herself knew of the pain caused when love and duty are equated by an act of squalid mathematics. It's arrogant to demand love; it has something of the financial about it. It was arrogant of the Nazarene to insist that he was the only one, way, truth, life, beard, sandals and all. But that's how monocults work, from Moses to Manson to Bhagwan and David Koresh. With pantheisms one has a choice. One tends to prefer, to varietise. One might have a better chance of finding love. But mono-deities are totalitarian and anti-choice: What have you got today? Well, there's God, God, God, God or God. This is the spiritual equivalent of the Moscow food queue. And we had music to match.

There was applause. Susan played an encore. Pathos, empathetic, ruled. The ghost of Philip Larkin haunted the

shelves while the phantom voices of little England quavered
forth. Brigit looked disgusted.

I rose and followed Clarissa from the dining hall, out
across the croquet lawn, past the statue of Albert The
Good, and caught up with her by a lily-choked pond. She
faced me, defiant, hands on hips.

'Why do you not love your family?' I demanded. 'You
would appear to be a most undutiful daughter.'

'I cannot love them. Even if I knew how to, I would
not.'

The sky darkened. Her eyes blazed. I was aghast, yet
horribly enthralled, etc. etc. . . .

The pathos of non-elective affinities. Family, god, nation.

. . . 'Then why do you stay here? What hold do they
have on you?' She ignored this question. 'Make love to
me,' she said . . .

'You must come again when there's better weather,' said
Marcia as she drove us to the station. 'It's such a shame you
couldn't use the pool today.'

Come and swim in our gene pool; a baptism to seal the
affinity.

Brigit stood on the platform. 'My fucking family,' she said. 'It's
just incredible. Under every stone I turn up there's some
religious freak. There's that old queen in the choir at the Abbey.
There's that arsehole Gregory who hates Australia and peddles
his shit round St Anthony's Oxford while his simpleton dad
tends to his 'vital' little church in Geelong and his mother hisses
on about blacks. There's the priest at Bourke who seduced my

mother – or was it the other way round? And my godmother sending me all those pious aphorisms and prayers on bookmarks. Fucking hell. Who will rid me of them?'

At St Leonards station Aleister Crowley had just painted over the nameboards with DO WHAT THOU WILT SHALL BE THE WHOLE OF THE LAW and was shuffling away carrying a dripping brush and leather travelling bag. (Why are famous heroin users also famous travellers? Crowley, Kavan, Trocchi, Burroughs, Richards . . .)

At Wollstonecraft Mary sat on a bench writing *The Rights of Women* while, next to her, her daughter scratched a lottery ticket.

At Crow's Nest the sky was thick with ravens and priestly currawongs, malignant angels. The booking hall was verdigris'd and castellated. Tombstones were embedded in the platform. Clarissa walked amongst them, in waistcoat and jodhpurs; she carried a hammer and a stake.

'My father is a vampire, like his father before him, and all the Earls of Inbredeen,' she explained. 'They will only make love to their favourite daughter. I am my father's favourite. This is why I am so pale. But I shall change this forever.'

'Brigit,' I said, 'how did your father love you?'

'Like you love a cigarette,' she said.

Beyond the city centre there is still a dead hour in the hills of the North Shore or along the flat untarred highways of the Outer West, stunning suburban sense of emptiness caused essentially by garages, i.e. there are no cars visible anywhere, moving or stationary, such that you feel self-conscious, doomed, the last car on the planet, the last person left alive. 4.30AM and the shift has cooled down after the initial frenetics. Zorba has left the mike and the Undertaker is on air covering all channels. Back in town they're queuing up to run the nightshift girls home from the funhouses and bickering about who's 'point car' on the Chalmers Street rank. After that, the sparse calls are punctuated by long stretches of silence. Some of the jocks run quizzes in the dead hour, when they're alone covering all sectors of metro Sydney, and Legion cabs become one widespread happy little cyberfamily: Who did Laver beat in 1960 ...? What is the largest land animal that is unable to jump ...? But the Undertaker is severe and silent between calls except to slag off drivers late picking up, drivers on radio bans and every other shade of misconduct with his rigorous, syllabically defined, military cemetery verbals. He sits there at base in his panopticonic cubicle with screen, mike, map and headset and his terse breath infects the airwaves and colours my vision of the city at night with a wash of terminal grey.

111

A call to assist a cabbie stranded at Five Dock with no jump leads. Then there's some rookie lost in the wastes beyond Campbelltown, took a wrong turn in Ultimo and ended up 60 k's south of the city: *Where did you say you were, two fer-five? ... What does the sign say? ...* **Don't** *speak to me in Chinese, two fer-five. Fer one thing it's contrary to the vee-haich-tee radio regulations of the State of New South Wales, feranother* **I** *don't understand it, and another thing I don't understand is what yer doing at Campbelltown and the* **Hagh-way** *when yer were supposed to be picking up in* **Manly** *half an hour ago, and wegottem them shouting down the line at us, two fer-five, so you are off air fer the next* **farve eours** *two fer-five. Caaronnaranket Punchbowl ferwunnagoder Mascot air* ... And then an M100 from Botany. For brevity or secrecy there's an M code for all the commonest contingencies, and this one means that some poor bastard has called in from Gloomsville asking about the 'M100 to Wollongong', by which he means he reckons his passengers might be about to kick up ugly. No doubt he's kicking himself for ever picking them up and meanwhile being extremely ingratiating until the cavalry arrives. Or perhaps he's the excitable type and knows little of conflict resolution theory. This would have been a more useful input at the Least-Cost knowledge school than all that no-fatty-foods-and-lots-of-exercise stuff. His location is relayed and a pack of the Eastern Subs' finest homes in to assist. Stay tuned for the outcome.

The radio work makes you a call girl but we're also street hustlers, and like these girls and boys – it's strange but the boys in their fishnet singlets cruise just off the main drag around a block of Darlinghurst hospitals and hospices – we're on the street too and we don't know who we're going to pick up. Sometimes first impressions are the wrong ones. I never once saw another cab stop for any of the groups of wino Aboriginals that hang about the inner city: *boongs* up ahead and out goes the for hire light. The soberest of the group will be hailing, and if you stop there's a five minute loading time while the walking wounded and plain paralytic are manoeuvred, cursed at and finally bundled inside, and then it's just a question of how many bottle shops we visit till they get service. They pay you alright, it's just that they hold you in the utmost contempt and make no effort to conceal it. This maybe is what some cabbies can't tolerate. Me, I defend myself with intellect, I get beside myself and study the situation. First trick in the book. It makes me wonder whether it was as this kind of basic defence mechanism, a distancing from immediate and/or emotional disturbance, that our race's self-consciousness first came into being, and that the quite accidental spin-off from this martial device were the various powers of human intelligence. If so, then nothing changes, from the fortified settlement which was the first building to the military today – which is still spinning off stuff at us for our minds and bodies to play with and thereby develop the human race, from Biros to thermal underwear to Teflon to the Internet. This blueprint for progress offers food for thought: is it horrific, delightful, liberating, necessary? We get threatened, so we disassociate to ease the pain, and while we're disassociated it's boring and we want something to do so we start analysing things, and *voilà hom. sap*. Next stop fire and the wheel, then watch this space for the life-or-death struggle of a little spheroid suburb lost between Venus and Mars.

Radio's been dead for five minutes which seems like an age as long as the Pleistocene.

So I don't mind getting the odd gang-bang from a bunch of winos, it's all part of the job. What sometimes makes it through the intelligence barrier is the occasional bollock-pissed power-suited Brit-hating schmuck, insecure like all nationalists, who talks at you with dry venom for half and hour and drops you off at the end of a bush track halfway to fucking Darwin twenty bucks short and more than a little ragged. It's date rape. Happens to whores all the time and they don't always live to tell of it. Meanwhile in global academia there's a bunch of spoilt campus brats crying lawsuit every time some frat bozo fumbles with their emotions. They should try the business end of the service industry.

Snaking down the Pacific Highway, which at this point is a built-up commuting route well inland, it occurs to me that one day the Pacific itself will be colonised, squeezed in a pincer move by California in the west and by the energy from its eastern rim; cyber industries on paradise islands. That is if the French have left it fit for anything.

Flying west from California to here, we've come beyond California, this is the bizarre secret. There is some remaining truth in the assertion that what happens first in the West happens in California, despite the fact that the state these days appears to be just a kind of drive-thru phase of a life plan, where you go in shit poor and usually from the south, make your bread and breed your brood, and after as short a time as possible break for the Oregon line and all points north on Interstate 5 for the free public beaches, decent life for the kids, the cool waters of Seattle, etc. In this way California is a kind of sheep-dip; it can be good for you, but those who linger too long are utterly purified by fire or madness.

Australia, too, is basically a Pacific coastal strip with a bunch of mountains and testing grounds behind it, a big influx of Pacific Asian peoples, plenty of wine and wealth, technology and suburbs, bush fires and earthquakes, big cars and cooking with noodles. It had outlaws and a gold rush and trouble with indigenes; it has fortune hunters, little heavy industry, beach and pool culture, maritime and gay activity, and exotic place names for the ruling English tongue. The highways are called highways and all roads look American; the cops carry guns, the typography of signs and licence-plates is the same and the plates are the same light alloy punched out in the state pen with the same state slogans: the First State, the Garden State, the Golden State.

But it's not a country which populations have tended to pass through. Rather they end up here, from the Aboriginals to the convicts to the postwar European and Asian waves. No one ever left Australia in droves unless it was to fight a war or microbus the globe.

Today the place seems to have the advantages of California without the associated hassle. It operates all the advanced modes of Western living without as yet having driven significant swathes of its inhabitants to the various exit doors marked *Abroad*, *Violent Death* or *Up Own Arsehole*. This may have something to do with one particular difference which is easily noticed by anyone who arrives here from the Reaganized/Thatcherized West expecting more of the same. Because for all its Yank brash, big suits and famous entrepreneurs, this is one nation that has bucked the trend and whose state still controls many key sectors, whose political colour is social-democratic, and whose labour unions are strong. So it is peculiar to arrive in a place where the Labor Party has been in power for nearly a decade, where there's a lot of cheap municipal public transport, where getting sick is inexpensive, and where the opposition Liberal (Conservative) Party is making zero impression with its alternative programme of more indirect taxation.[1] There has been plenty of deregulation here, especially in the financial field, and Australia has even been described as having

---

[1]With spectacular imcompetence, Liberal leader Dr Hewson is making the promise of *more taxes* the *main plank* of his campaign. Needless to say, he will shortly be pasted at the polls.

'the world's first Thatcherite Labor Party'; nevertheless this is not somewhere ravaged by monetarism to such a wholesale degree as the UK, and unlike California the disadvantaged are not yet being thrown to the sharks or left to turn their guns on each other.

All this to the immense frustration of our loud neighbour the Brit expat, he who regularly repines to his dinner companions on the subject, and who has clearly been deeply shocked to arrive in a country where those nasty ideas *society* and *community*, only *–isms* away from utter degradation, still have a certain meaning. Thatcher proposed the family whilst disposing of society, but the fever didn't catch on in a country where 'bastard' is a compliment; and where single parents, officially known as 'lone' parents in the UK, are instead called 'solo' parents, with less connotation of the outcast (in fact it sounds strangely and appropriately athletic). Perhaps the colony's very founders, for the most part men forcibly separated from their families by transportation, were necessarily more alive to other forms of collective bonding; the many trade unionists and politicians among them obviously were. This isn't any kind of communal Utopia, it's creaking at the seams like anywhere in the West and if it hadn't got lucky with minerals it would be bankrupt, but it has an extraordinary stability like its icons: the monolithic Meccano of the Harbour Bridge; the huge, ponderous brown base of the opera house which anchors those white sails to the rock; and slap in the middle of the country there's a distinctly immovable and irresistible red hillock that everybody worships. Even the outrageous foot of a kangaroo is a monument to stability, as is the much-loved and spectacular stasis of the koala.

I thought I was alone on this six-lane highway, speeding down through a steep cutting towards the Parramatta River, but an ambulance has overtaken me. It's moving with some haste. It's a tall white van, British-style, with a window in the back the size of a giant TV screen. Oddly, this window isn't curtained or sufficiently tinted and for a few moments I am able to see, in a lurid green light, the scene inside that it frames, which is the head and shoulders of a person in a smock, propped up at an angle, staring forwards. I watch this figure from the same point of view as the viewer of Mantegna's *Dead Christ*. I can see the scoops of the shoulder blades, the sinewed neck, the rictus of the jaw, the thick black hair, the wide eyes, the pale shock of some sudden enormous sickness. I take the person as female, middle-aged, but it's hard to tell. I don't know whether the face is frozen in anger, or despair, or fear, or whatever permutation of anxiety, but one thing it isn't is resigned, not quite. She's still hooked up to instruments, the electrodes, the dripfeed. I can see the shoulders of those in attendance on either side. Then the image rapidly shrinks and the ambulance is gone. Ambulances and hospitals make me feel vulnerable. They tend to bring on sudden aches and pains. Touching base with my bones. Mortality reporting in, alive and well.

With physical injury there is usually a consensus reality to rely on, but with mental torments and disturbing behaviour everyone has a theory, if not a say. Fogs up the screen somewhat. The one that prevails by the skin of its teeth goes for the mechanistic, inherited chemical-imbalance stuff (like – it's only alcohol that's killing Abbos, they're not made for it . . .); says it's really just a physical dysfunction, and has some correspondingly physical solutions involving regular workouts at Joe Mengele's fitness centre (or Redfern Police Station).

Brigit herself believes the opposite, that is all physical injuries have mental causes, from cancer to a cut finger, and she argues it well.

I tell her that when a crow shits on you out of the blue and

117

you start chasing psychic teleologies for it, this is not medicine, this is chaos theory. You may trace the route back from the township wiped out by that hurricane, and continents and years away you may even find that very lepidopt who started it all, and then what do you do? Pin it to a cork and root out every butterfly on the planet? This is not medicine, it's revenge.

So often, she attempts a medicinal revenge on her family: from bittersweet memories she isolates a moment, is sure she's found the key, to their nature, to her own; but her parents' granite reality is as elusive as a butterfly.

Me, I believe in unlucky accidents. As well as those Gravesian bright bolts. Like Brigit, this bushfire blonde of mine.

But I'm flying on instruments here; I'm improvising. I've done it all my life. I've always felt extemporary. That's why I've come here, looking for accidentals, modulations. Improvisation depends on choice. Growing up, I was spoilt for it like any other kid in the postwar West: spoilt for occupations, spoilt for partners, and I made an effortless transition from teenage love to serial monogamy, which amounts to the same thing (this is why rock 'n' roll became more than a youth culture: don't ever want to lose that beat). But I'm stuck for experience of this kind. I never loved a woman this unhappy. The abreaction I did recognise, because strangely enough a couple of years ago, not long before I met Brigit, I saw someone curl up in a chair in front of me and begin talking like a two-year-old, and when I turned to leave the room to fetch a (strong) drink, she began to bawl out don't leave me, don't leave me. Later she explained she'd thought I was her father and that I was leaving for ever. Her natural parents had left her to adopters at the age of two.

Which is why it is strange to have now seen the same thing overcome Brigit, right down to the identical and anguished pleas. Is this a new vocation calling me, or what? It's a lonely business dealing with someone in depression. They are not themselves, and they don't see you as you: you become their parent, and as such a focus of opposition and denial, else of breakdown and supplication. Normal relationships are suspended. It's easy to swallow the chemical imbalance theory because so often the low mood kicks in like the throwing of a switch, like a quick-acting personality changer, alcohol on an empty stomach. Once the switch is thrown, adult logic fails, and the adults get frightened. And so the search becomes for some counteractive switch to throw, some immediate antidote: volts or drugs.

I succumb to a yearning for the uncomplicated affairs of my past: women who were ecstatically happy with their fathers, women who had learnt how to employ benign contrivances in order to get their way. Bat your eyelids at Daddy is the fundamental formula. Women who know what men like about little girls. This kind of father figure I can play. *Love, the sledge that smashes the atom? No, No! Antagonistic cooperation is the key* . . . as Carlos Williams has it in *Paterson*. I'm not happy with the confrontational bullshit, the backdated bloodletting.

Along the deserted Parramatta Road at Leichhardt a wide shadow steps out from beneath a colonial awning and flags me. I pick him up. 'The Cross.' Here's someone else after an uncomplicated affair.

Yeah, women who hide stuff. Almost like prostitutes hide themselves. This is less complicated. Not pain-free, but the anxieties are simpler ones, the deceits are real rather than imagined.

Swinging into William Street, there's that ever-mounting world population figure again. This is the wrong place for such an announcement, especially in sight of somewhere specifically dedicated to non-procreative coupling. A better way to get this post-industrial message home would be to display it in every residential district, or permanently in the corner of everyone's TV screen. Meanwhile at the Cross the pre-industrial party goes on, just, crawls towards the dawn. A drunken French girl is tumbled into the back of the cab. 'Get her home mate, she's got the address on her.'

Brigit isn't part of the monogamous series, however. To her I made a life commitment. Would I have done so if I had spotted this on the horizon?

No mate, says a voice in my ear, you'd have been off like a bride's nightie.

Oh yeah? says a voice in my other ear, what about love and lust?

I've got a devil on one shoulder and an angel on the other like a fucking Popeye cartoon. Got to hand it to the devil, though: he was first on the buzzer.

I should have spotted it. Godalmighty, I'd just done a test run with someone else riddled with family-generated insecurities. I wasn't up to that. I must be just ... tailstruck.

Who was it sang *something for nothing / is everybody's plan*?

French girls are so polite. This one's almost paralytic but she's doing her best to puke out the window. I haul her out at the youth hostel in Glebe. Some vomit has managed to blow back in so I'm going to shoot back to base and clean it up.

I'm parked outside the rest room at the edge of the forecourt while I swab down the vehicle. Up until a week ago this room was a lowlit and rather shabby affair that hadn't been touched for years, with a row of sepia-framed photographs on one wall depicting various golf matches from the forties and fifties between the different Sydney cab cooperatives, the teams lined up in their plaids and plus-fours. Then a film crew came along to use the base as a location, and for the sake of a big new picture the framed memories disappeared, brilliant white emulsion was sloshed everywhere and strip-lighting installed to give the place a sufficiently bleak and hard-edged look. Art leads life. Which is only right, of course.

The base is deserted at this hour but for the odd driver zipping in and out to refuel. Among them is Otto, a talkative Czech and unemployed mathematician. He always seems to know everything that goes on. On his way out he drives across to me, compares our earnings so far this shift (the bastard's always ahead of me), then points out a cab parked over by the wash bay and asks if I remember that M13 back around 3.30. So that's why radio was dead for a while. I hadn't noticed when it first went because I was carrying a bunch of students from Newtown who were partying with their INXS tape. Otto says, 'You know Kev, the new Irish boy?' I do, I gave him a lift to work yesterday. An optimistic teenager from Belfast who'd just emigrated to get out of the rain and the Troubles. 'It was him, up at the Cross,' says Otto, 'Got a nasty customer, some cult or other, dark suit, knifed him, you know, really badly, no reason, no provocation, and he's on a life-support machine at St Vincent's. Terrible, man.'

'Did they get the guy?'

'Not yet. But they towed the cab back. Take a look at it before you go. See you at pay-in.' And he's gone. He doesn't seem too worried on his own behalf. I guess he's already run an actuarial check on the situation.

So I cleaned up, filled up, lit up, and went over to the blue Falcon. Holy shite, they must have sliced through every artery he had. I don't envy the cleaner. The blood has shot out everywhere – windows, seats, instruments, ceiling. I can smell it and it makes me retch.

Could have been me. Or could it? Was this just crowshit, an unlucky accident, or could someone else have avoided it? Were there psychic butterflies involved? To hell with philosophy, I need some fresh air, I'm out of here. Half a minute later as I drive up Albion Street a Japanese man steps out of the funhouse and hails me. He's shivering in his lightweight suit. I take him over the bridge to North Sydney. All the way he's saying, 'It's cold, it's cold.' I whack the heat up but it makes no difference. 'I'm cold, I'm cold ...' Sounds like Snowden in *Catch-22*, moaning in his flak jacket.

Now, somewhere high above Lane Cove, racing along in the sodium-amber darkness which coloured my infant nightmares, the sugar sweetness of the Camel cigarette will do for mother's milk.

It's coming on to rain, the screen's fogging up and I can't figure out the de-mist. The Undertaker is droning on. Fuck him. I kill the radio and hit the tape. Thelonius flying on his instruments.

The obvious difference between jazz and straight Western music is the fact of improvisation. Jazz imported from pre-civilised culture the idea of free action within a defined field. I think of this field as unenclosed pasture, as opposed to the Western tradition in which everything is defined and the land is enclosed like the city, grid-mapped; like the civil project, within its limits nothing is left to chance, every note, every direction, every street is predefined. In this way the jazz soloist by contrast is a nomad, a hunter-gatherer. The territory here is a series of harmonic progressions; there is a beaten track – a stated theme – from which it soon becomes essential to wander, down less-beaten paths or along ways previously untrodden. Even the limits of this territory can be mutated by use of new chord inversions, superimposed intervals, sevenths, sixths, thirteenths: bebop like physics insisting that space can be curved, bent. Blues bending notes. Jericho's walls falling to the Israelites' nomadic horn. One hears much about the expressive possibilities in Western classical music, and one sees masterclasses and concerts where individuals sweat buckets to achieve their own personal rendition of a piece within the formidably limited parameters allowed by notations so detailed and determined that as little as possible is left to chance or whim. Yes, there *is* more than one way of hitting a particular piano key with particular volume, dynamic and expressive at a particular moment as defined by the score – just – but consider the effort this takes to achieve, the angst of the soloist, and the never more than minimal difference this makes to the piece, which remains triumphantly intact. As the hero of hard-boiled fiction has it: 'I hit town yesterday. It didn't feel a thing.'

At the mid century, John Cage addressed this problem on behalf of the classical tradition and showed he could go one better than the jazzers. He chucked it all out, got rid of the enclosures, wiped out the grid plan; moreover, he abandoned regular rhythm. He had no trouble losing that beat, much to the puzzlement of many jazz musicians who admired so much else about his project, which talked of freedom and benign purposelessness and was linked to a political agenda which was quintessentially American in its individualism. But Cage could afford to lose the beat: his tradition was a cerebral one and he was looking for nirvana.

Brigit has found hell and looks to the beat, the shimmy, the rattling of bongos to save her. For me there can be a near perfect balance of perfect terror and perfect joy in this driving rhythm, this dark, feet off the ground, flying on instruments, in my ol' Ford Nirvana, egoless in hell.

I looked up *ecstatic* the other day in the dictionary. It comes right before *ECT*.

There are a lot of Mediterraneans in this cabbing game. The Lebanese in particular run much of the industry (and the belly-dancing business too for that matter). Levantine excitability is at home on the Pacific Rim, on par with cabbies all over the oriental Pacific. There are cabbies who talk at you manic, rapido, nonstop, like some gypsies will. The angst of the cabbie requires constant sweetness, comfort foods, cigarettes, argument; produces races against time and petty deceits for the sake of petty radio fares. Keeps them bickering with the radio boys, preventing work being called and thus winding up everyone else, keeps them running red lights, cutting you up for street hails. Something gut-bottom keeps them on the roll, incessantly moving, tongues, wheels, eternally combative. It's some nomadic urge. But this is bound by the city, and the whims of strangers, and the obligation, contradictory to the spirit, to always be working while moving: hence the underlying nerves. And with it this strange, predatory condition: out there in the dark there is nothing worth considering, just commodities, punters, and I'm just moving through it with the shit arrogance of a Tartar through Muscovy. I value the settlers only in terms of exploitation. It's not real out there. I see it all through a screen, I hear of it via radio waves. It's just TV. TV, to whose condition all art now aspires.

Wherever I go I like to see how people contrive to move themselves, whether it's an old woman in a Zimmer frame, a boatload of refugees or someone taking a cab. To keep still is really a very alien state indeed. Very other-worldly. Most meditation postures are designed to keep the body as still as possible. This seems to be necessary for certain mental or esoteric excursions. Hence the beatless Cageian project. But this is a heavy discipline, and it must be so because it is opposed to a primal fear of staying in one place for more than an hour or so without at least a visit to the kitchen, the lavatory, the schoolyard, or even just across to the window. We tend to timetable ourselves to ensure that we remain in constant motion. Is this why examinations are so fearsome? We enter an examination room as if it were a railway terminus or an airport. We take in our prepared equipment, we bring with us keepsakes, mascots, and comforters, and lay them out as if on a tray table. We turn the experience into a journey.

And then that final 'journey', that contemporary Western death, slow and communal, which has us grouped in a semicircle of high-backed chairs facing a giant screen, as if on the flight deck of a starship. The screen, from whose colourful bourn no traveller ever returns. In the end, TV takes us all.

We've reached a state of simply going round and round in cities, the 24-hour drive time, just running on the spot, barely able to contain the urge to up and away. Still afraid of that nasty old African rift valley sabre-toothed tiger. And the fear peaks at night: we're still and vulnerable, and it's dark and the big cats are abroad. The tooth and the claw, the Cross and the switchblade, the bloody cab.

This primitive urge to keep moving was subdued, controlled and contained by means of the civis, the city state – a place (and an idea) defended by bricks and supplied by industry; and ever since this neolithic revolution the greater part of populations appear to have had an increasingly limited mobility – you get phenomena such as the imperial Russian *Propiska* (still in place post-Gorbachev) where a city wall becomes less for preventing entry than for prohibiting exit. And you get the fascinating reactions when gypsies penetrate Europe in the late Middle Ages: these people have always been seen as a severe threat to the settled population, and no doubt there were race memories of Huns and Golden Hordes in operation too; but there was the other side of the coin: there might be protection from a king, there would be a 'superstitious' awe of the exotic and the paranormal attached to these wanderers. In parts of India today there are groups of itinerant musicians, notoriously mendicant, who are both despised and regarded as holy. Gypsies would also

125

come to occupy superior positions in our sexual imagination, either as desirable or predatory, or both. This ambivalence is also reflected by a pub in north London, the Gypsy Queen, where beneath its painted sign of a fabulously bedecked and desirable woman, the handwritten notice *No Travellers* taped to the window.

Then with the advent of railways the age of mass mobility was born, and now your average Westerner travels more than ten thousand miles every year by car alone. The urge and the ability to travel for the sake of it seems to be greater than at any time in recorded history, and has made neo-nomads of us all.

Tourists really are very advanced people. But ever since the mid-nineteenth century when the railways gave industrial workers a week at the seaside and Thomas Cook gave the bourgeoisie package tours of the Continent they have attracted extraordinary levels of hostility and contempt. One extreme example of this is the slogan that appeared on city walls in the 1980s: *Tourism = Terrorism*. Hostility to tourists takes many forms and is evidenced when the species is met both at home and abroad. A hundred and fifty years ago when restaurants in Italy began serving British dishes to cater for their visitors, this landmark in multicultural history was viewed with horror by intellectuals. Intellectuals today accuse tourists of creating 'non-places', 'pseudo-places' wherever they go: places such as airport shopping centres and 'traps' like Covent Garden, Darling Harbour, or the French Quarter in New Orleans.

In the 1840s the poet Wordsworth tried to prevent construction of the Kendal–Windermere line for the sole reason of preventing tourism. The man who had done so much to mythologise the Lake District in his poems and guidebooks turned jittery when the masses began to show up on his doorstep for a piece of the action. He didn't consider their sensibilities worthy enough for the privilege of travel and wrote

'Artisans and labourers, and the humbler classes of shopkeepers should not be tempted to visit particular spots which they have not been educated to appreciate.' Ruskin agreed with him and could not abide the thought of people getting drunk among the fells and daffodils. Likewise the tourist today is considered to have an insufficient ability to understand the host environment. They are accused of pausing only to take pictures and never long enough to really appreciate the phenomena they come into contact with, when of course they merely have a different take on these things, a different sensibility.

Those who despise tourists are at pains to use another label for themselves when they go holidaying: 'I'm not a tourist, I'm a traveller.' This reactionary view of tourism is composed of varying degrees of envy and elitism; it parallels the attitude to gypsies, and boils down to an issue of cultural conservatism, of neophobia. Today's 'traveller' has inherited the tradition of 'going native' (R.F. Burton, T.E. Lawrence, Thesiger – going native appears to be particularly popular when natives are nomads) to a greater or lesser degree, their goal being to disturb the host culture as little as possible. What is constantly bemoaned is that this darling little backwater, in whatever corner of the globe it may be, has been changed forever and for the worst by the coming of tourism. What is particularly reviled is the way tourists will overlay their home culture (and/or global 'Coca-Cola' culture) onto that of the host – from fish and chips on the Costa Brava to Budweiser baseball caps in the Amazon – and through this interaction throw up a mutant crossculture of events and artifacts born specifically from the relationship of visitor and host. The 'traveller' tends to prefer cultures to be both static and discrete. The tourists themselves, and the locals who cater for them, don't give a shit for this, and rightly so, since so many static, separate or separatist cultures have had a habit of coming to sticky ends either by generating wars, riots or revolutions, or by being ill-equipped to cope with change forced upon them from without. The clearing of rain forests has hit previously intact, pre-civilised peoples like a sledgehammer; the actions of nationalist governments continue to have similar effects on their people and their neighbours. Compared to other social enclaves, and demonstrably in their own right, those dedicated to visitors from abroad tend to be models of international and crosscultural cooperation. The only good ghetto is a tourist one. There are exceptions to this – segregated beaches in Mexico, paedophile brothels in Thailand – but these examples are not inherent functions of tourism. The art it throws up, from hybrid versions of ancient native practices to theme parks and plastic ashtrays, to particular representations of a place's 'heritage', may be subject to aesthetic and political contentions and considerations, but this only adds to the pleasure. Two of the most delightful phenomena of contemporary travel: the fact that in so many tourist spots it is not a local you will be dealing with, but someone from yet elsewhere on the planet there on a working visit; here in Sydney, for example, the visitor will be hard put to find a nice Australian girl in some of the classier bordellos. And then there is the idea that millions of people have been to thousands of different spots across the globe and have all brought back an ashtray made in one particular corner of Asia: thus all souvenirs have become souvenirs of Korea. The search for the authentic is as futile as it is irrelevant: the situation is too liquid.

In the afternoon I'll come home wondering which Brigit I'll find, the authentic one or the possessed one who leaves me twice as lonely as this endless trail of tarmac and crumpled dollars and fragments of lives. And I still wonder if I'll find her alive. Out here on the road, loneliness can at least recognise and engage with itself; time slows and the dead hours last years.

Indoors the situation is too fluid, too fast, I have trouble reading the signs, trouble adapting. Too often I don't make allowances, under the fond illusion that if I act normal it'll go away. This loneliness arrives by stealth, under false pretences. Sight fails me, touch fails me, words fail me, instruments fail me: *Insufficient memory *Press any key to continue* – in the same old vein, that is.

I can feel the blindness of this love over which we wear a prosthetic intellect, a complex scaffold, like that which wraps the Centre Pompidou or the London Lloyds building. And in the centre of such an immense and instrumented superstructure is this tall atrium of desire, this well of air and light with a Reading Gaol's eye-view of the sky.

Hyperreality in Bourke Street, 7am Sunday morning: at Bourke and Liverpool I pick up three tall, glamorous women and am directed to the Taxi Club, just half a mile up the hill but it must be hard work in those heels. Then as we pull away I realise they're not women but transvestites. And a minute later, after closer scrutiny I realise they are indeed women (the small thyroid cartilage is a giveaway), but they are women dressed as men-dressed-as-women: thick make-up and husky voices and a certain T/V sheen. This is reality cubed; this is T/V^2. The girl next to me has made herself a Marlene lookalike; her long tight-fitting dress, her bespangled cleavage, her 'dahlinks'. Marlene was the queen of T/V^2. She paid her camp male fans the extraordinary compliment of imitating *them*; she became woman dressed as man-dressed-as-woman; so this here Marlene lookalike has gone even further – she is T/V^3. Where will it ever end, where will it e—ver end?

Older Australians still enjoy a good bit of cultural T/V – they still like to dress up in the garments of the mother country, like a child rooting in mummy's drawers and trying on underwear. The Harbour Bridge, 1932, Dorman Long, is an imperial suspender belt, and gives the appropriate thrill. The flag, a British naval ensign, is the garment with which they staunched their wounds and shrouded their dead. And how they love a parade, with all the Emperor's old clothes on view.

Meanwhile the children wear authentic English Doctor Martens shoes. The fashion has just hit and there is Air-Wair mania on the streets. The schoolteachers don't like this and some have already banned these hyper-ordinary, practical, sensible, unostentatious and comfortable items as if they were the flashier fashion of an earlier generation. Why? Unostentatious is the giveaway – Docs are *cool*. And they have unacademic associations with art students, skinheads and factory workers ('Guaranteed oil, alkali, and petrol resistant'). And being imports they are expensive. Most of all, they are cool items *disguised* as mundane footwear, and teachers are beginning to double-take just as I did with the girls in the cab.

Here's where Docs bend the gender: it's the girls who want them most. They want to wear what are men's shoes, the Docs which are a complete disavowal of centuries of notions about what a female foot should look like. Lightness, narrowness, pointedness, embellishment – every last remnant of footbinding goes out the window. Girls from seven to forty-seven all want to be low-heeled trannies. And if they're fashionable, then they must be *sexy* . . .

'All I can say is how dare they sell a man's black shoe to an underage child who knows no better.'

'I find it faintly disgusting.'

'They look so old-fashioned – isn't is a bit necrophiliac?'

'Yeah, you get a skinny lovely in a pair of Docs and it's like rooting a boy.'

'Or a nurse.'

'I can't bear them! I'd never wear them, they're so unfeminine. I mean who do you hope to attract in them?'

Who indeed? And of which gender? And would that matter?

You can draw lines of sexual division in any number of ways.

AUSTRALIAVILLE

The line which was based on the supreme Need to Breed occasioned by the neolithic revolution, and is now somewhat redundant to say the least, is now being contorted or erased by endless degrees of mimicry and counter-mimicry in what is a charming game of flirtatious hide-and-seek, a lovers' foreplay, a game of mirrors. Now there are not just sexual black-or-whites, now there are mulattos, quadroons, octoroons and the possibility of every exotic shade of grey under the sun – but all teasingly concealed beneath glitter and denim and fishnet and pneumatic-soled shoes. As for the Emperor's old clothes, be they union jack, barristers' wigs, military memories, political deference and other such cultural garments, they have become so worn out that they are completely transparent. This is not a pretty sight.

'"Here! You may nurse it a bit if you like!"
the Duchess said to Alice, flinging the baby
at her as she spoke.'
Alice in Wonderland, Lewis Carroll

Colin Sutton, a short, thin man in his
early fifties dressed in yellow polo shirt, blue jeans with knitted
belt and big white sneakers, stoops down to yank up a small
green shoot from the black earth. He examines it mournfully.
If his already long jaw – which gives his face the appearance of
a tanned parsnip – were to drop any further it would bury itself
in the crumbling loam at his feet.

'This should be nine inches high by now.' He shakes his head
in despair. 'It's unreal, this drought.' The tiny wheat seedling
with its inadequate roots wilts between his long fingers. Behind
him in the distance white grain silos glare above a rusty morse
code of servicing freight wagons. All around him, the huge
plain, endless as Kansas or Iowa; flat geometries, immense
skies, desiccating heat, the dark earth like powdered chocolate.
Another bad year in store for the farmers.

But Colin needn't worry that much. He's in what you might
call a sitting position. He used to farm 600 acres out near Dalby;
had good few years, collected a pile of health insurance (nerves

133

and knees), sold up and retired at the grand age of forty-nine. Now him and Paulette have got a bungalow back up in the cooler mountain airs of Toowoomba, and they've got an '86 canary-yellow Falcon with big black roo bars plus a little trailer in the garage for those customary neo-nomadic excursions across the continent. We are on a lesser excursion, out west from Toowoomba to the Suttons' old haunts on the Darling Downs (black-and-white photos from the Brownie Age come later). We've seen Beef City (smelled it long beforehand, an invisible fog of sour Bovril) where the Herefordshires walk Spanish under the corrugated towards the man with the electrode ('They had to fire the previous bloke. Used to say a prayer for each one of them. Slowed us down.') and the semi-trailers hauling their skinned and hollowed forms off to Japan. We've watched the Cecil Plains cotton gin churning out big white cubes of protomarblewash, and picnicked in an enclosure by the factory wall and seen off a panhandling roo. Now we're heading for the folks who work what used to be Colin's neighbouring six-hundred.

Dan and Connie's place: a simple two-storey house of peeling white clapboard, stilted above garage space (a common flood precaution), standing in a small, open yard. Connie appears at the top of the steps. She's wearing blue jeans and white sneakers like Colin and Paulette, except they're a few degrees grubbier. 'He's not there at the moment I don't think,' she says. She means the local koala – the rest of us are craning our necks to scan the branches of the tall gum tree which overhangs the house. As for Dan and brother Pete, they're out in the fields, so we set off in the direction of a distant ute and a couple of crouched figures, and in a minute or two we're all gathered at the spot where Dan and Pete are squatted at the junction of two irrigation pipes and fiddling with wet cement. G'day, g'day, g'day.

Dan and Pete's attire is several stages grubbier than Connie's: the greasy patinas of their floppy fisherman's hats, T-shirts, shorts and boots are a medley of terminal greys. Colin and Paulette also sport floppy hats, but crisp, white and pristine. Brigit and Colin are the only ectomorphs here, and you can tell they're of the same blood: Colin's weatherworn face, deep-set beady eyes and wiry limbs make him the spitting image of his sister, Brigit's mother. The others are all big-boned, on the plump side. A languid conversation follows as the seven of us stand in a circle and stare at the dry earth and the puny shoots, every so often squinting up into each other's eyes, talking of drought and rain and how to use what little water there is available. Boots and sneakers prod the soil. Arms are folded, heads are sagely nodded. Phrases like 'I know, it's a worry' and 'Still, we just got to hope for the best' are soothingly uttered. No one's panicking. They're in a groove here. It may be unreal but it's nothing out of the ordinary, yet.

A couple of fields away is an expansive rectangular earth-work, a low ziggurat that goes by the name of a Turkey Nest Dam. From the top of this reservoir's bevelled banks you stare down (quite a way down by this time in the dry year) at a square lake dotted with duck and stocked with fish. Our party has come over and clambered up here to take up previous stances and continue its gentle murmurings like a strange *a cappella* chorus shyly praying for rain.

Pete is the serious churchgoer. He's tall, and squints down benignly at you through pebble-lensed spectacles. He asks me how things are going in Britain at the moment. I give him the lurid version. Pete is surprised. 'I thought Margaret Thatcher was supposed to have got things shipshape.' Brigit begins a gently corrective teach-in.

We are at the very beginnings of civilisation: this wide plain; these strict geometrics of fields and tracks, ziggurats and pipes and lines; this flat-earth society; those mountains to the north and east. We are in Sumeria (the Darling Downs are as young). We are at the dawn of number, of accounting, of linear time. Of permanent settlement: the hunter-gatherers driven out to the harsher west, the nomads forced back to the mountains. We are at the moment when Cain kills Abel – Agriculturalist Slays Wandering Shepherd – and goes on to build the first city. We are at the moment when Gilgamesh overcomes Ishtar – Disaffected Customer Slays Brothel Madame – and the race of women joins that of the nomads in a slow and steady slide. The moment when this fusion of events – agriculture, bureaucracy, homocentrism, commodity, murder, the city and hence the state – sets civilisation in motion on its awesome course across the millenia. Fasten your belts, please, and tighten them too – there are lean times ahead. The walls are going up. Division of labour is rearing its specialised, fragmented head. The priests take charge and invent the recording of history with reed and clay tablet. The demoniac engine has begun to turn (7000–3000 BCE).[1]

When settlers from the south began populating the Downs in the 1840s they had long ago dumped Ishtar, and Enkidu's[2] curse on the harlot –

You shall sleep in the desert
You shall stand in the shadow of the wall
The thorn and the bramble shall wound your feet
The drunken and the thirsty shall smite your cheek

---

[1] See John Zerzan's essay, 'Agriculture: demon engine of civilisation' in *Apocalypse Culture*, ed. Parfrey, 2nd edn (Feral House, Los Angeles, 1990).
[2] Gilgamesh's ugly factotum.

– had turned to reality and was thoroughly endorsed by the new white regime: remembering that harlots (f. Latin *caro*, dear, hence whore, harridan, hüren, etc.... and chère and Charles and Caroline ...) were dearly exalted in Ishtar's day. But it was still a Mesopotamian reprise: yardsticks and grindstones, the construction of gridiron settlements and cities; priests who were also judges and lawmakers; and over in the heart of the machine, here are the first farmers, out on the hot wide plain. They believe what they read in the *Daily Tablet*. They'd better. They feel a bit *exposed* out here. You can't hide on the plain. God has your grid reference, and everybody else can see you for miles too.

Dalby is a crossroads town of a few thousand souls, two wide and dusty main streets, and a lot of colonial corrugated. Down a small side road, on a hedgeless lot, Paulette's parents live in a simple chalet-bung built on blocks, and we arrive here at sundown for sweet tea and chocolate biscuits. Sat around the table in the trailer-like kitchen, I imagine I'm in Worthing or Cromer or Dawlish, in the days before reflective numberplates. Paulette's father is a massive man in an old brown suit. His gleaming, bronze-bald head looks armour-plated; liver spots have totally colonised the backs of his huge hands. He's distracted, and somewhat deaf, and gives everyone the vaguest of acknowledgements. He's had some heart trouble too. 'Not what he was,' asides his organised wife. We're still on our first biscuit when, prompted by Brigit, he begins to recount the old days: the travel, the trains, the police, the riots ... but most of all the routes: Alpha, Jericho, Barcaldine, Longreach; Middleton, Boulia, Phosphate Hill; singing the map of his life, a map drawn on sandpaper. Then he held his jacket aside to display a good-sized paunch. 'Now this ain't a beer gut – I don't drink anymore. This is from shearing. This is where you hold the animal, and it's rubbing, and it causes this layer of tissue to build up inside me belly. Like leather it is. Badge of me trade, this. Marked for life.'

Think on our received images of those long-off and lovely salad days in early Sumeria. Everything is clean and neat and tidy as a colouring book, no sweat. Beautiful, square-shouldered young men in loincloths work with lifting and boring equipment, with oxen and ploughs. The irrigation canals are sky-blue, the healthy crops a brash viridian. Tall, dusky maidens in silk and sandals carry elegant water vessels to and fro; a man with tunic and beard stands before a pile of bulging sacks and carves figures into clay ... *alles in Ordnung*, everything tranquil as a suburb ... all this collective harmony is somewhat reminiscent of German National Socialist paintings (*Land, Farmer Plowing, German Earth*, etc.) or Chinese posters of the 1970s ('Win a good harvest – increase grain production', 'Put your heart into farming', 'Brigade chicken farm', 'Well-drilling equipment built by a commune', etc.). A tanned, bare-chested demi-god works the sluice wheel at the Turkey Nest Dam; a ute draws up and some Cleopatra lookalike emerges bearing a tray of wine and grapes; and as we leave Dalby we see the accountant in tunic and sandals and tablets under his arm stroll down main street as Aquarian sylphids bearing amphorae on their heads cross the road in front of him; he smiles through his long pointed beard ... no worries.

Brigit is determined to discover as much as she can about Colin's childhood with her mother, their upbringing, their early life. She's trying to find the many missing pieces of the biographical jigsaw that her mother is unable to supply (perhaps because of self-censorship, perhaps due to whatever mental damage may accrue from half a lifetime's use of lithium). What might have caused a beautiful, sparky, twenty-five-year-old Australian girl to attempt a Plath-like death in a London lodging, and survive barely intact, held together from then on by Jesus, toxic drugs, husband, motherhood? Was it Daddy, Daddy you bastard ...? Well, let's have a look at the bastard. At the kitchen table (blue-flecked yellow melamine), under a heavy duty neon strip light, Colin has fished out a picture from a box stuffed with snaps: Circular Quay, *circa* 1940 – here's a big, broad man in army captain's khaki standing smiling for the street photographer. He has his arm around each of the kids: Margaret is tall for a twelve-year-old and is radiant in her schooldress, while her younger brother is short for his years and looks pretty serious behind the smile. Perhaps he had a premonition; this was the last time they'd see their father.

'He just showed up out of the blue one day,' says Colin. 'I hadn't seen him since I was a baby. He wanted to see us before he shipped out.'

Pat Sutton was a wanderer, it turns out. His first job involved a trip to Gallipoli. Once demobbed he did the outback rounds – shearing here, droving there, selling automobiles in Perth for a while, encyclopaedias elsewhere, zig-zagging it across the country during the twenties. The nomad flirted with civilisation long enough to marry a Sydney girl (no photo; beautiful? She must have been to keep him tied to a shack in Balmain for four years) and produce three kids. But when she died shortly after giving birth to Colin, the wanderer departed again: kids weren't enough to keep him tied down. He just vanished one day, hit the highway alone and grieving, and left civilisation to deal with his offspring. The kids spent the thirties and forties in a succession of separate homes and hostels in New South Wales and barely clapped eyes on each other, let alone their father. During this time the elder boy, John, climbed his way out of a Parramatta orphanage and was not to be traced for another thirty years. Pat Sutton survived the war, so the records said, commanding machine-gunners in North Africa, but nothing was seen or heard of him again.

'He's probably still tramping around out there somewhere,' suggests Brigit.

Colin's eyes have welled with tears. 'I bloody miss my brother,' he says. He's choked. 'I missed him all those years ... and then to finally meet him and find out that he's ... and it was like a slap in the face, Brigit, a slap in the face. Wasn't it, Paulette?'

(John lives in a house in Camperdown, Sydney, with his friend Teddy.)

Colin has turned deeply morose. Paulette doesn't exactly confirm the blow to the face, but she puts a comforting arm around him, pats his shoulder. 'What did I do to deserve it?' he moans.

'Hang on a minute,' says Brigit, 'let's get something straight —'

What she gets straight is that Colin blames his 'nervous breakdown' partly on his brother's sexuality, which is supposed to go against nature, etc. etc., and have helped render Col fit for nothing but (Paulette's words, in an aside) 'mooching around the house, doing the cooking and watching the television'. (Paulette's a great socialiser, always out at bridge, golf, the WI ...)

I doubt that a medieval inquisition could have dispelled Colin of his unhappy notions. Brigit and I had a go for about an hour (even Paulette weighed in once or twice) before realising this. But having the conversation then steer towards the state of the national economy proved a useful tool to buck up Colin's spirits, and in no time at all he was laying heatedly into all the bludgers, the layabouts, the workshy and the government handouts that were running the country into the crowd. It was like a market day in the pub at Newton Abbott. You know the song: Spent My Life On a John Deere Earning a Living from the Sweat of My Brow, While Some People Don't Know the Meaning of Honest Toil. The Sharecropper's Lament, best sung from a sitting position.

'Don't knock Colin,' said Brigit later, 'I hate it when you do that. He's the only one of my family who isn't a religious fanatic, and Colin and Paulette have told me so much stuff that no one else would.'

We hit the coastal strip – fertile and dotted with little mountains – after a three-hour meandering drive northeast down the dividing ranges past Lake Somerset. We are on our way to visit the cover star of this month's *National Pig Farmer* – Brigit's cousin Kenny – and Colin and Paulette have their trailer in tow, intending to stay over a few nights. The small communities strung along the coastal highway north of Brisbane have the land well under cultivation – sugar cane, bananas, grain, fruit and so on – but they are suburbs just the same; there's hardly a stretch of road without a township, a cluster of houses, or just a gas station in view. Ease of communication with a city defines a suburb. By these standards of modern transportation and telecommunications even the Darling Downs are not remote enough, nor sufficiently uncultivated, to be called rural (there are too many right angles – another yardstick by which to distinguish the *civis* from the *pagus*).

This country is famous for being predominantly suburban. But the suburbs too are early-civilised models. The fields and smallholdings of the neolithic revolution appeared before the cities which eventually sprang up in their midst. Cain first tilled the ground in a suburb. The German word for suburb is

Vorstadt, before the city, in space and time; immediately pre-civic, the fore-state. And think of sub-urb, below the city, in terms of archaeological strata. These criteria also make suburbs of large swathes of territory such as lowland Western Europe or the Midwestern United States. The rural is banished to mountain, desert or tundra. You can live in Camberley, Surrey; Hope, Arkansas; Berlin-Charlottenburg or Nyngan NSW and do it in the same style. The global suburb.

If this suburbanism is a reversion to the very earliest form of civilisation, then the next stage back is nomadism. Consider the activities of civilisation's senior citizens in countries where they have the wealth and the space: what they want to do most is jump in the Winnebago and traverse the continent, and they combine road travel with time travel by buzzing up and down the consanguinitic highways in every state library's genealogical department. Look at Colin and Paulette and their trailer. What have they worked for? What has been the meaning of their life, the goal? What do people want to do now when they can afford to quit the treadmill? They want to hit the road (though until this moment many have retained a jealous hatred of Gypsies, who always refused the civil whip).

Colin and Paulette's bungalow is simple and unextravagantly furnished, and they cultivate nothing save a basic lawn front and back. They attach more importance to the fixtures and comforts of their trailer than they do to their house. They spend six months of the year on the move, and when they're not travelling Europe, America or Southeast Asia, they're busy caravanning Australia. This is what the height of civilisation has eventually produced – a population which first aspired to the suburb and, having obtained this, now yearns for the nomadic. It begins to resemble an escape.

This escape has ancient precedents. The simple scheme of 'natural' progression from nomadism to settlement to western industrialism advocated by traditional anthropology has recently been losing its credibility. We know for example that between 1000 and 1500 CE, Amerindian civilisations such as the Anasazi, the Mogollans and the Mississippians had developed and urbanised the land, and subsequently abandoned their civil project to take up hunting, gathering and horticulture. There seems to be no evidence that this 'reversion' was caused by catastrophes such as large-scale wars or pestilence. All that remains are the mounds, irrigation systems and sandstone cities. They lie there in their mystery, like the forsaken meal on the dinner table of the *Marie Céleste*. Perhaps their inhabitants simply got bored with the civilised menu and jumped ship. A similar case can be made for Asian pastoral nomadism, i.e. that it originated amongst settled stock-breeders who subsequently took to the open pastures at the end of the second millennium BCE. It might also be asked what led the Gypsy people during the Middle Ages to abandon their homeland in the long-civilised Indus Valley and take to the road.

Young Kenny is big like his mother and quiet like his father. The small, shabby colonial bungalow stands half-ringed by neighbouring canefields and is upwind from the close-by piggery. Kenny reeks, however, of organic overdose and politely stays a couple of paces away as he greets everybody on the lawn. 'Still got that bike, Briggie,' he says, and directs her to a shed where she has a happy reunion with the trail bike she rode around on seven years ago. Indoors we meet Kenny's wife. Her name is Wendy and so she is called Wendo. 'G'day guys,' says Wendo. Wendo is not as tall as Kenny but she's built just as solidly, bejeaned and slightly bow-legged. She was brought up on a cattle station out west and still prefers horseback to motor car. At first I thought she was carrying a small sack of oats but it turned out to be a baby. It looked kind of incongruous. It looked even more incongruous an hour later, clamped to her tit as we sat round a table in a bizarre pub on the highway. Imagine the House that Jack would have Built had he been legless on the Foster's, and you have this three-storey timber atrocity with roof awry, floors-a-sloping, balconies akimbo, bars awash and a busy little restaurant. A Krazy House designed to get you in the mood before you've even slipped and stumbled your way across ramp-like floors to the bar. An extravagant joke for tourists. But the curious thing is that at the Krazy House, the more you drink, the more sober you become. This is why the locals avoid the place; and why we drove back for supper all earnestly discussing the state of the national economy.

Kenny's a young agrostar. He can get a generation of prime porkers conceived, born, weaned, fattened and off to the electrodes faster than anyone else in Australia. He's still just a tenant-manager here but he's being headhunted by the industry's big boys. It seems hygiene is his number one priority: sprinkler systems, elaborate guttering, block-free drains, frequent disinfecting. You've never seen, amongst the immaculate geometries of breezeblock and steel tubing, pigs so clean. You can hardly smell them for the Jeyes. They're pinker than Spam. Kenny gets Brigit to pose with a suckler in her arms, like Alice did in Wonderland. In obliging, Brigit looks about as happy as Alice (in Tenniel's picture the heroine is seriously contemplative: is the piglet she clasps to her chest a symbol of her generation's offspring who would grow up to plunge Europe into bellicose turmoil in the first decades of the twentieth century?)[3] On our way out past the weaning pens Kenny plucks

---

[3] See Francine Lineker's study of Victorian culture, *High Psychedelia* (University of Nebraska Press, 1991), which identifies a golden age of hallucinogenic endeavour, defined by cultural workers who were users of

out a couple of half-dead runts and consigns them to the incinerator.

Towards the end of supper the pressure is turned up on Brigit as she sits next to the still-suckling Wendo: 'I expect you'll be embracing motherhood soon, Briggie ... you're ripe for it, girl ... ah, yerl just love it ... it's what it's all about ... give her the baby, Wendo, she's dying to hold it!' Brigit forces a smile. She doesn't want a child. She's only just had a termination. But she doesn't care to announce this as the bundle

---

hashish, opium and every other *pharma* in the *copoeia*, and giving us a glut of inspired, lunatic fantasia in every artistic, spiritual and literary form, from H.P. Blavatsky to St Pancras Station, *The Lady of Shalott* to Richard Dadd, Dickens, Balzac, Berlioz, the Brontës, the Pre-Raphaelites, Romantics and orientalists. Lineker views the first edition of *Alice in Wonderland* as a prescient lament to this age: 'Carroll knew the end was coming. The Alice books are works of high psychedelic nostalgia, framed by their archly poignant dedicatory verses ... When Alice takes the pig and stands there embowered by foxglove and wild grasses she is clearly possessed by a vision of the future. The dream would soon be over. The machine age would control the totality. Sherlock Holmes would make his last stand; creative drugs would soon all be outlawed. Official art would be limited to that made with the aid of coffee, tobacco and liquor – drugs of the banal, drugs of the crudest geometries, drugs favoured by lobotomists, priests and lawmen. Alice's shell-shocked eyes gaze to a future where the free manifestation of human exaltation will be proscribed for the final assault on History's summit, where all the horrors of the age lie in wait, from the Bauhaus to the battlefields and concentration camps; music would be reduced to twelve narcissistic tones gazing in a mirror; the realism of the retinal would rule, and deeper intuitions be condemned as degenerate. She saw what the camera was already doing; she saw what Carroll and his circle were producing with it. No more superimposed fairies and intimations of other worlds; instead we have stark, skinny pubescents with bare pudendas – before *Readers' Wives* came these *Readers' Daughters*, like refugees from Haight-Ashbury in the last days of 1967.'

is pressed upon her. The bundle knows, though, and begins to bawl. It turns into a piglet before my very eyes.

'I know,' says Brigit, after we're abed in a sleeping bag on the living room floor, 'but you didn't see what it turned into after that – and after that. I nearly puked all over it. Yeah, that's me, the Vomiting Madonna.' An unforced smile which then turns wan: 'Be no problem if I knew I didn't want kids. But I don't know. Everyone's so fucking insistent.'

So was the bundle, which kept up an all-night wailing, keeping Brigit tormentedly awake till dawn. My own soporific brain ignored the cries and to- and froings of Wendo and I slept well. 'Yeah, you would, wouldn't you?' says Brigit disgruntedly, '... well at least we know where one of us is at.'

We have reached the time and place of earliest civilisation where women have not yet been utterly coerced into the specialised role of breeding machine, but soon will be as the growing industry demands more human grist. Nevertheless most people are rooting for it. This is what Enkidu's propaganda is about. Marsden's too. Priestesses and concubines and women dedicated to culture and pleasure must now retrain for a career in babymaking else be thrown out and reviled. The dear woman, caro, chère, harlot, is relegated to the shadow of the wall and the bad breath of legless punters, or to a temple of love bristling with panic buttons, two-way mirrors, monitors, security guards and power-dressed madames who forbid socialisation with your co-workers after hours – your average Surry Hills house of fun, where the drunken will still spit in your face. That's the line. Wendo is going for it in her butch, one-of-the-blokes fashion (Wendo because it's appropriately masculine); Paulette has come through it alive and relatively unscathed; and Brigit is passing through, still holding out, having experienced satori with *The Female Eunuch* (famous cover like a Beef City carcass) somewhere between Uluru and

with brigit in sumeria

Adelaide: she came down from the red mountain, drove to Alice, climbed on the train, opened the book, and read it through. After this, she didn't speak for three days: 'I just wandered around with my mouth open, staring at people.'

We said goodbye to Brigit's family the next morning and took a hire car south on route 1. On the way we passed the Krazy House. 'It's like one of Kenny's photos – did you see them? All skewiff – all of people pissed, or taken by people pissed,' Brigit observed, looking up from her journal as the pub flashed by.

Some of the freeway was spanking new, but it was just like any other freeway; the model hasn't been improved on since the autobahn. The years which produced the autobahn were a watershed. The universal, ten-thousand-year-long civil project of which superhighways were just one element – this peaked with Hitler and Stalin, who took it as far as it could go before disappearing themselves to the music of splitting atoms. The former went like Gilgamesh, surrounded by suiciding deputies; the latter was entombed like a pharaoh. Since then such pre-civilised elements as individual travel, feminism, psychedelia and neuroresearch, sexual publicity, ecology and pantheisms have helped initiate the post-civilised age. So also have civil elements of both healthy and toxic nature, but a lesson can be drawn from Mesopotamia, cradle of monoculture and its appropriate -theism, and civilisation's prototype. Since this extremely time-consuming experiment has been a bit of a fuck-up from day one to this, from Gilgamesh to the Gulf War, it's clear that Gandhi got it wrong, and that a little less civilisation would be a good thing. Don't believe the propaganda of those pretty pictures of Olde Sumeria; certainly the fields were lovely and the crops grew tall, but they are not full of Kirk Douglases and willowy maidens – those men wear floppy hats and dirty stubbies, and have pocked faces and muddy boots; and the

147

women are plump and weatherworn and wear trainers with built-up heels. And in the nice village street they've got a hunter-gatherer drunk and are kicking his head in; while at Government House, Cain's boys are running the scene. Cain – they call him 'Sugar' in these parts – gets away with murder. Still others dream of packing up this year-round slog and heading for the hills again – they're bored with sitting around the house reading Bradman's biography (and very pissed off that his average was only 99.9); give a farmer half a chance and he reverts – or should we say progresses – to nomadism. So respect to Colin and Paulette, Falcon and trailer, post-civilisation's finest, there in the vanguard.

'In civil business, what first? Boldness; what second and third? Boldness: and yet boldness is a child of ignorance and baseness'

Francis Bacon

Regulation green metal fences, four-foot high (the Twombleys have one) are appearing around domestic pools. Their sudden appearance in a lush back garden instantly municipalises the landscape.

What has happened is a rush of reports of babies and toddlers falling in and drowning: POOL DEATHS – NEW MOVES. Some want pool fencing to be made compulsory. Others call this a stupid, expensive over-reaction. Others want swimming lessons. The first group wins and a law is passed. Shortly afterwards comes a stream of amendments and exemption clauses, hard fought for, and the battle rages on.

The pool fence controversy brings other arguments to mind. The new laws are an hysterical reaction (ignore the suggestion of female here), like the drug laws. A handful of casualties amongst a vast ocean of activity is deemed an excuse for blanket intervention. And the sex laws too – these derive from Jehova's act of hysteria (certainly no suggestion of the female here) in the Garden of Eden. Like sex and drugs, the pool means pleasure. It's a little suburban Eden. People hang out here with little or no clothes on. They take booze, grass, coffee. They have sex. Ahem, Commissioner, we've got to fence this place off, fast. – Why, Reverend? –Why? Because there's a millionth of a per cent of a chance that at any moment a tot may drown.

As far as safety is concerned, choosing pools as an issue may

151

seem a trifle arbitrary. Consider that hereabouts your car doesn't need any stringent safety test; and that on Sydney's railways rush-hour masses pack into ancient trains called Red Rattlers[1] whose sliding doors are long defunct and stuck permanently at wide-open: this doesn't raise an eyebrow.

But with pools, babies are involved. It's reminiscent of those other issues involving abortion, artificial insemination, etc. Bodily, intimate, personal, domestic scenarios. Drug-taking, abortion, sexual behaviours, private pools ... the control fanatics and pushy moralists move in with the most spurious of excuses to mark the limits. To fence us off from ourselves.

---

[1] Some of these trains have a destination board which reads, aptly, MUSEUM.

At first it's like the Welsh border country during a summer drought. Leafy cattle pastures where the greens have mostly turned to mustard browns. Clapboard farmsteads, Friesian cows. But then there are gum trees, flocks of dirty pink galah birds, and bony Indian oxen with shoulder-flaps and dewlaps. We're inland from Byron Bay, approaching the McPherson range which straddles the Queensland border.

Vicky stops the four-wheel-drive hatchback at the first of a series of cattle gates across the road and asks Byron to get out and do the gates. 'I'm not old enough,' he protests.

But the pale blond boy is forced out to do the business. Half a mile ahead a forested mountain rises suddenly from the grassland. Vicky is worried about the transmission and checks the oil. Then we hit the rudest of dirt tracks and hairpin it upwards, crashing along at unfeasible gradients through the ruts and debris. Halfway up at around a thousand feet we stop to look at the view – palms and gums, conical mountains clustered all the way to the horizon – and I take a picture of Vicky and Brigit. Vicky is the taller. She's a lean, sun-bleached blonde who favours ancient denim. These two are used to going up mountains together since they trekked through the Himalayas eight years ago. This here mountain feels more like the kind of Welsh or American one that might have some variety of artist or hippy on top.

153

AUSTRALIAVILLE

The mountaintop as enlightened location. Site of earthly paradise and/or a Wise One who imparts the Meaning of Life. Example, Hassan I Sabbah and his hashishin of Alamout; the Old Man of the Mountain got them stoned, showed them a garden of unbelievable beauty, and thus motivated a series of political murders against his enemies back west. And all those other old daddies who went up the mountain and brought down the law.

Zion – Olympia – Rushmore – Valhalla – Mount of Olives – Castle Dracula – Calvary – St Michel – Fujiyama – Pisgah –

The first mountain you ever climbed taught you a great truth. It was Snowdon by the easy route (Llanberis/Pyg Track). As you reached the summit, the café closed.

52.Kên/Keeping Still, Mountain. The hexagram turns on the problem of achieving a quiet heart. It signifies the end and the beginning of all movement.

As in a dereliction, a solitude. Muhammad, Kerouac. You go there to gather, you return to spread. You go to get the Big Picture and you come back with your blockbuster in the can: Commandments, Korans, Thus-Spakes, Zen Chautauqas –

Thank you, I think we have the picture. Brigit and Vicky balance precariously on a log, arm-in-arm, as I capture their souls.

the trees in paradise

At two thousand feet a stilted house is perched in the lee of the summit, shaded by eucalypts and tropical fronds. It's constructed from solid chunks of brown timber. The build of its owner is similar. McDonald's cropped hair and bushy moustache recalls Gurdjieff or Nietzsche. Or Merv Hughes. Up on the deck he welcomes us warmly. He embraces Vicky and shakes hands with the flimsy Byron before giving the boy an order and handing him a broom. The kid whinges. McDonald growls. Vicky heads for the kitchen. The kid sweeps. Brigit and I lean on the rails and gaze out through the trees and across the rolling mountains to the distant ocean, and we breathe the scents of paradise. Marijuana is rolled and we smoke the smoke of McDonald as he describes his subtropical Eden. We are surrounded by bird-of-paradise flowers; strange bunches of knife-like leaves exploding, undefeated, from charred stumps; the echoing of bird calls; a liminal blue mist, and strong light shafting through the canopy to illuminate twisting trunks and patches of fibrous forest floor.

McDonald's voice rolls engagingly over us. He is talking of firewatching, bush-fire science, how the vegetation is adapted to survive conflagrations, the lie of the wind, the frequency and pattern of fires, the watchers' systems (he is one) and their rude equipment and means. The first subject of paradise: inferno. (Is this how the Old Man of Alamout taught it – the precariousness of Paradise, the necessary sacrifices?)

A couple of miles below is a grey homestead. 'See much of your neighbours?' Brigit enquires.

'Fuck the neighbours,' says McDonald. 'I come here to be on my own. Fuck the community. Damn community can't even get its firewatch act together. They won't fork out for the phone lines.'

Vicky comes out and serves up a Waldorf Salad. She's getting skittish, doing little dance steps, singing snatches of tune.

'Can I stop sweeping now?' – a plaintive request from the boy Byron.

'Where's the dressing? You forgot the dressing,' complains McDonald. 'Jee and we waited long enough.'

The naked lunch is eventually dressed. We learn more of McDonald. Thirty-seven, born Sydney, Cromer Heights, schooled at an Anglican college. Surfie, carpenter. He got this place built by presenting it as a project for architecture students. As we talk about the house, Byron, sat apart at his own little table, asks about some insect landed on his plate. McDonald addresses him severely: 'Byron, you do not interrupt other people's conversations. You should know this by now. And if you really have to do so, you do so politely. You say "excuse me" and you wait to be asked to speak. I've told you this before.'

The kid is muted.

'His mother doesn't control him enough,' McDonald confided to me later. 'Vicky's so undisciplined. All over the place.'

'Ever seen a lion move in on a partnerless female?' I said, 'First thing it does is go for the cubs. Kills them with a single snap of the neck. This get's the lioness's hormones going instantly, it really gives her the hots for him.'

'Ah, Vicky's got no problem with her juices,' said McDonald, and thought some more. 'I tell you what though, it would save me a lot of hassle. I've got no time to bring up that kid. It's a mother's responsibility. She's going to have to accept her duties. She's far too soft on the kid, too. He's a damn wimp.'

Down on the slope Vicky and Brigit were imitating bird-of-paradise flowers, limbs akimbo.

McDonald didn't appear to lead a very sociable life. All the friends he spoke of were in countries overseas, as if they were his agents. (The dagger falls in Cairo but the orders come from Paradise.)

*

Inside, the house is loungy, well cushioned. Panelling and furniture from recycled timber, lovingly polished au naturel. A poster depicts the serene and celestial ecstasies of paragliding: against a butane-blue sky the padded figure descends like a prophet or a terrorist. Old toys – model cars and trains – on the shelves. A black altar of a hi-fi. Carpenter's Heaven.

Access CARPENTERS . . .

The humble terraces of St Alphonsus Road squats, Clapham, 1977 – young carpenters everywhere, lying on platform beds, stripped floors, sofas built from old joists; plugged into J.J. Cale and Ruddles Ale. Secure in their anatomists' love for the guts of a building. Constructing extraordinary conversions, attics, galleries, knock-throughs . . . and hierarchies. The carpenters ran the street. There were two or three chiefs who had beautifully converted lofts, chic bedmates, a light van, and a plan. And they had numerous followers who lived lonelier lives in humbler rooms and constantly struggled with the fixtures and fittings, their provincial anxieties, their uncertain ambition, their need for a leader, their political angst, their old bicycles and lack of cash; and who were willingly exploited by the chiefs as cheap donkey labour on jobs for gentrifying architects or, on more glamorous occasions which involved trips to Devon or Powys, stints building or rebuilding the remote hideaways of successful pharmaceuticists. Hideaways built from scratch or from derelicts, stone barns or A-frames, but customised, and always extraordinarily contrived from a carburation of wild ambition and psychedelic euphoria, choke-started

157

with brute force. Hideaways just like this one, whose owners were big chiefs, often bigger than the carpenter chiefs, and with the most glamorous and untouchable bedmates – no match for the clumsier hedonisms of the thick-wristed crew...

Vicky leads us upstairs through a hatch and into the loft where a large bed lies before a tall pointed window which stretches from floor to ceiling and gives out on the awesome panorama of green mountain range. She kneels on the bed, gazes out, sighs with pleasure. 'Jee this place is so beautiful. Isn't this just the perfect bedroom?' We admire a slickly-jointed beam with polished pegs. Byron is hustling around our feet with his broom. 'Byron will you get the hell out of here with that bloody broom,' snaps Vicky. 'Why do you keep following us around all the time?' Byron turns a translucent shade of pale and pipes a protest as he is expulsed via the hatchway.

Vicky lives in a brand new suburb (no town attached) that Alan Bond has put down over a cluster of rolling fields north of Byron Bay. Closes and crescents and chocolate-brick houses in the close embrace of transplanted palmery. Down the road, a little harbour with pelicans and fishing boats; over the hill, the long white stretch of Pacific beach. Grundy's Australian dream.

Vicky does graphic art and helps produce the local newspaper, and lives in a two-bedroom unit on the first floor of a condo. She would much prefer to live a forty-minute drive away in that earthly paradise with the Young Man of the Mountain.

'He's a bit of a fucking sergeant major,' says Brigit.

'I'll iron him out, don't you worry.'

'Fucking hell Vicky, you were about as assertive as a dishcloth up there.'

Vicky giggles. 'I know, it's the grass.'

The TV's playing back-to-back pop videos. Vicky knows most of the Australian musicians personally or intimately. She's tended to pick her men from the rock-drug-art-surf milieu (Byron's father is currently doing time for transporting heroin), and the ones she has chosen have all tended to knock her about some. But she reckons she's through with all that. 'I've grown up since having Byron.'

'Do you still go to church?'

'No, not really. Christmas and Easter . . .'

Vicky's a lapsed Catholic. Holes left by the departure of the faith's more fanciful aspects are now filled with astrology and other such fancies; but the dominate-me core appears to have survived. A framed illustrated story in the bathroom, R.C. Repositoryesque, tells the popular tale of 'Footprints in the Sand' which explains that the Lord is always with you and when He's not walking beside you, He's carrying you.

She would go and live on the mountain on McDonald's terms. The kid would do all the character-building menial stuff and keep his broom out of the bedroom and basically be not seen and not heard if he valued his cervical vertebrae. Meanwhile Vicky would slowly but surely turn her master into somewhat less of an anachronism. This seemed to be the plan.

'I should keep off the grass then if I were you,' is Brigit's advice.

But Vicky's eyes have gone dreamy, and I can see her doing anything for her man – tightening up her waitress act, sending the kid off to boarding school, letting McDonald knock her about a bit, or playing Governess for him and spanking his botty with a hairbrush. I close my eyes with holy dread. Vicky is the poet who has seen Xanadu, she who 'on honey-dew hath fed/And drunk the milk of paradise'.

The trees in paradise are fireproof. Is this a good sign, or a bad sign?

He was going up to his aunt's place to shoot roos. Standing by the bus, in the heat and glare of the station precinct at Dubbo, wrapped in a cheap fur-lined jacket, smiling through his scraggy black beard. 'Yeah, better than hanging around unemployed in Sydney ...' He'd been on the dole for fifteen years, ever since leaving school. He cracked another can of Victoria Bitter. 'I got to get away from my mum every so often or she'd drive me spare.'

On the road to Narromine he said he was a good shooter but he didn't have a licence. 'They make roo licences rare as fucking hen's teeth. My aunt's the only allowed. I use her gun.' Then he gave us a lowdown on wrestling kangaroos: 'You got to get them by the tail – it upsets their balance ...

'... Yeah, I got an uncle. His farm I suppose. Be doing a bit of fruit-picking you know ...'

Brigit asked him if he had any cousins.

'Yeah, I beat up my cousin when I found him smoking dope. He's a karate dan he is.'

'You beat up a karate dan?'

'Yeah. I mean, I went for him, didn't I?'

'Get him by the tail?'

'It's principles. I didn't beat him, obviously. But I don't like dope. It makes me weird.'

'Was he forcing it on you?'

161

'No, no.'

'Maybe he likes it.'

'I tell you, just one puff on it and I see spiders crawling up the walls.'

Brigit raised her eyebrows: 'Oh really? That's very interesting. Do you know that the spider is a well-know symbol for an overbearing mother?'

But he'd lost the plot and was repeating the jazz about getting roos by the tail. Rat-arsed, he stumbled off the bus at Narromine to go do his hunting and gathering. 'Bye, thanks for the chat.'

'Watch out for those spiders,' said Brigit.

Route 32 is a two-lane blacktop which runs west from Sydney and ends up a thousand miles later in South Australia. A hundred miles west of Narromine, via Trangie, Nevertire and Nyngan (dusty old towns reminiscent of places in western Kansas) the accompanying railway peters out near the mining community of Cobar. They mine copper here, and the dirt on nature strips and vacant lots is the same colour. We left as darkness fell. The next town is 150 miles away through the bush, and there's nothing on the road but a very infrequent truck or road train stacked high with sheep. No side roads, no homesteads; and the sky is a vast dome glutted with stars. Periodic glowing yellow diamonds flash past, reading STOCK or FLOODWAY; those which warn of kangaroos are ludicrously unnecessary, since the beasts can be seen lining the road in their thousands.

They come out to feed at the verge between dusk and dawn. The heat-retaining tarmac is attractive. It's also lethal. The road is strewn with their corpses, decapitated, partly mashed. Every other minute the bus, now pussyfooting it, must swerve to avoid yet another freshly struck national emblem, a great bleeding bale of flesh and fur, while its companions squat nearby, nibbling at the meagre, burnt-out grass, raising their heads to greet the glare of our headlamps with their character-istic nonchalant, no-worries-mate expression. Not a problem, they seem to say as we round yet another ponderous victim, there's plenty more of us where that came from.

'Plenty' is an understatement. In this corner of the state alone there are currently ten million roos bouncing about, which is five times the normal amount. A glut. Farmers hate them because they're thriving in a drought year and scoffing grazure and water needed for sheep; so they've had to send many more of their herds prematurely to the abattoir. Good for the meat-eating public because it's at giveaway prices in the butchers', but just loss-cutting for the farmer. A glut? More like a plague.

What about a spot of mass culling, then? Get every able-bodied unemployed Aussie out there blasting away till the problem's solved, with the bonus of all those resources: roo fur, soft and warm; roo hide, excellent leather; and roo meat, lean and tasty (they say the Germans love it). A welcome bounce to the economy. But it's not that simple. As well as the shooting restrictions there are only a handful of small operations licensed to process carcasses and these have a strict and minimal quota. These limitations mean that your dead roo is good for nothing but in situ fertiliser. And so far the policy is sticking. Country people blame the green lobby, along with misguided national sentiment which is squeamish about killing a totem animal. Cuddly roo-toys are OK and the souvenir shops are brimming with them, but real roo skins are much harder to find.

There is also a glut of national symbols today. Apart from the sacred roo, there's the emu and the koala; there's the shape of the national map, there's the Southern Cross, the Bondi lifesaver, Uluru, Sydney Opera House, lyre-bird-and-sun, the Aboriginal flag, Ned Kelly and Crocodile Dundee. And every other day some new design for the national flag is touted: the Union Jack is withering away like a redundant umbilicus, but with what to replace it?[1] There are more choices than roos. So many identities to choose for the maturing nation.

Five more hours along this highway of carnage and we can see the distant lights of Broken Hill. At this point another well-loved emblem appears: the pissed okker in a flatbed ute, meandering and lurching ahead of us. The driver, silhouetted in our lights, is wearing a large bush hat. The town has sent out this native guide to pilot us in. The truck slews off into a ditch, swerves back across the road into the other ditch, and every so often manages to steer a straight course along route 32's median line. Thus is the highway of identity negotiated.

Brigit didn't see it quite like this.

'They drive the same way in Ireland,' she said. 'It's a well-known sign of an overbearing mother.'

---

[1] Traditionalists are loath to let the UJ go for fear that it will leave a black hole in the sky – black as Italian hair, or Aboriginal skin, or bean-curd soup.

I was beginning to get very tired of sitting on the rank, and of having nothing to do: once or twice I had peeped into a book Brigit had lent me, but it had no pictures or conversations in it, and what is the use of a book, thought I, without pictures or conversations?

So I was considering in my own mind (as well as I could, for the hot day made me feel very sleepy and stupid) whether the pleasure of blowing smoke rings would be worth the trouble of lighting up a cigarette, when suddenly a young woman in a white pullover and pink ribbons in her hair opened the passenger door.

There was nothing so *very* remarkable in that; nor did I think it so *very* much out of the way to hear the girl say severely: 'You're late! Get in!'

I thought she must be with a companion I hadn't noticed, or a small dog or something; but this was not so. She was on her own. She got in and settled herself. I started my engine. 'Where to?' I asked. At this she gave a furtive sideways glance.

'Where to?' she asked meekly.

'Station,' she replied promptly, severely.

We were soon bowling down Oxford Street.

'What time is it?' she suddenly asked, and began to fumble with a wristwatch she had pinned to her pullover.

'Quarter to one,' she replied sharply. 'You're *late*!'

165

'I know, I'm sorry,' she said.

'You're always late,' she admonished.

'Yes, yes, I know, I'm sorry,' she said.

We pulled up at the lights at Taylor Square. She glanced at her door. 'Get out here?' she enquired, then looked at me.

'No, this isn't the station yet,' I said.

'No, not yet, you fool,' she cussed.

'Not yet,' she acknowledged.

Curioser and curioser.

This passenger of mine had two distinct voices, this was clear. But not two minds, as far as I could yet tell. I was hearing a dialogue between the directive and the executive parts of a single mentality. There was no conflict involved, only severity and submission.

We stopped again at the lights at Riley Street. She began to fumble in her purse. 'How much is it?' she said.

'We're not there yet,' I told her.

'Put your money away,' she told herself irritatedly.

'Right,' she said, quietly complying.

Was this the mentality that built civilisation? The hanging gardens, the ziggurats, the libraries and the pyramids? Some people think so. Julian Jaynes speculates that until the middle of the first millenium BCE humans had no ego, only a directive/ executive personality.[1] A bicameral mind, with one part ordering and the other carrying out, without question, those orders. And they heard these orders, the voice of God told them what to do and they went to it. Breed those babes, plough those fields, build those silos and cities, export that grain – and then

---

[1] Julian Jaynes, *The Origin of Consciousness in the Breakdown of the Bicameral Mind*, 2nd edn (Penguin, London, 1993).

eventually, different cultures clashed: news of other lands, other gods.

The characters in the *Iliad* rush around Troy like autom-atons, with their gods telling them what to do at every stage. They don't introspect, or ponder this advice. There is no guilt: if reproached for a slaying, a hero states that he was only obeying divine orders, and this explanation is accepted. But by the time of the *Odyssey*, things have changed. Troy is in ruins, and other civilisations have lost their totalitarian grip. Wars, migrations, national disasters, refugees are on the move, populations are intermingling. People are hearing conflicting orders. Which one to obey? Are any of them to be trusted any more?

And wandering around the chaotic Aegean, Odysseus becomes *wily* Odysseus, able to prevaricate, procrastinate, dissemble, deceive, make up his own mind. The gods direct less of the action amidst all these migrations, enslavements and kidnappings. Odysseus is out on his own in the wake of the Dorian invasions, to survive you needed a subjective conscious-ness. From the collapse of civilisation's initial rigid structuring and certainties, the human ego is born.

This young woman was a relic. She had walked out of a past when to hear was to obey; what's more she was broadcasting the very process – I could hear the call of the Dominus from her right lobe, and the response of her executive from the left. Did all Mesopotamia once echo to the sound of these internal dialogues?

The lights turned green. Bicamerally I obeyed and throttled the cab forwards. Cues, automatic responses, square-bashing, hierarchy, was this all there was in Sumeria? Musing thus, I was suddenly visited with an historical explanation for a recurring nightmare I used to experience around the age of four, one which had intrigued me ever since. The dream is composed of two scenes: in the first I am standing before a railway signal whose semaphore arm is at 'halt'. My sister watches as I demonstrate the correct procedure, viz. when the arm leaps upward I proceed, chuff-chuffing and pumping my arms, and when it falls, I come to a halt. There is an abrupt cut to the second scene, where I find myself observing a long corridor stretching away in both directions. The corridor is dark, and faintly bathed in an amber glow.[2] Along it comes my mother, running for her life, face contorted with fear, pursued by an unseen terror – but it is clear that this pursuer is awful, dark and male, and bent on the woman's destruction. At this point I wake up sweating. Am I being given two snapshots of life between the rivers, *circa* 5000BCE? Signal Obedience, and the Great Mother on the Run? Ti'amat pursued by Marduk? Was I being given, in my post-infantile state, a little Welcome-to-Civilisation message from my collective unconscious? Coded instructions to toe the line or else be pursued by Enkidu-the-Ripper?

'What yer got *those* tights on for?' she snapped.

Without being conscious of it I had hung a left at Whitlam Square and now we were barrelling down Wentworth Street.

'Others are in the wash,' she replied.

'You've got the ugly ones on!'

'I know, I'm sorry.'

'And you're late, you're always late.'

'I know. Damn. What's the time?' She inspected the watch again.

'Five to one. You're *late*.'

'I'm *sorry*.'

I was following the White Rabbit, that cussing and fussing

---

[2] Amber – 'Stop only if it is safe to do so'.

bicameral slave to time and lackey of bloodthirsty aristocrats, down the rabbit hole of Wentworth Street.

Alice's Odyssey, over land and water, confronting bizarre monsters, automata-like creatures and confused beings, refugees from a scattered empire, people making fumbling attempts at logic, or with merciless, murderous designs (Off with her head!), is truly Ulyssean in its stream of emergent consciousness. After the bicameral baby books – A is for Apple, B is for Ball, See the ball! Throw the ball! – flat statements and imperatives such as drove the protagonists of the *Iliad* – comes the journey of the emerging ego, full of inquiry, pliable, but not prepared to put up with bullshit, and necessarily rebellious ('Thinking again?' says the Duchess. 'I've every right to think,' says Alice), since her life is more than once threatened by the Kali-like figures of the Duchess and the Red Queen. Alice prevails, and survives – and not without the help of a wide selection of psychoactive drugs: we see her ingest everything from laudanum to cannabis tincture to psilocybin to hash cookies; and we can see that *look* in her eyes.

Jaynes's angle on the history of civilisation has been criticised for omitting to consider the role of psychedelic plants as ancillary to the liberation of consciousness, as antagonistic to monoculture and the crude mechanics of the civilising process. Neither does he dwell upon how bicamerality might have been originated and developed, nor suppose that, previous to this mentality imposed by the civil project, paleolithic humans may have possessed different and varying configurations of mental processes which may or may not have included a subjective ego. Some groups may have seen gods everywhere and in everything, and flown with them on mescalin ('switch off the internal dialogue' is the *brujo*'s command) and travelled in Odyssean landscapes, making inventions and cultural advances as they went; others may, like some present-day nomadic groups, including gypsies, have had little or no concept of deity at all; then again, the exploitation of suggestibility, which is what bicamerality boils down to, may always have existed to a greater or lesser degree. Today's civilised people still insist on a rigid conditioning process for their children and to a large extent their peers; but news from elsewhere travels faster today, and if people want to tune in to their next-door-nation's TV party, they will. The diehard civilised can now only survive – if this is the right word for it – in highly regulated, isolated, fortified or quasi-totalitarian communities – compounds like Koresh's Waco fortress, Amish hideaways, Chinas, Paraguays, Jerusalems, Baghdads, Tehrans: neo-Uruks, Babylons, Troys – Sylvania Waters, Double Bay. …

I pulled up outside the station, and she pulled out a handful of coins: 'How much?'

'Five dollars,' I said.

'Five dollars,' she said sharply.

'Five dollars,' she said. She placed a dollar in my hand.

'That's one,' I said.

'That's one,' she said.

'That's one,' she said, and placed another dollar in my hand.

'Two,' I said.

'Two.'

'Two.'

'Three.'

'Three.'

'Three.'

We got there in the end. Chiding herself once more for her tardiness, she got out and hurried away down the tunnel.

The girl had a double condition: first, she had no ego, and second, she was broadcasting the fact. The external world was her 'ego', and she took her cues from it. No doubt she had been instructed to take a cab to the station; possibly there was not a single action she took on her own initiative. Was this condition congenital, or caused by injury? Or was it possible she had been brought up to somehow miss that post-infantile Odyssey necessary for the development of a strong subjectivity? (And was stuck as young children often are, in the 'reading aloud' phase, to boot.) Our education system still seems to produce a surplus of bicamerality, the kind of call-and-response stuff that is fine for budding machine operators, simple transcribers of language, and other slave-like occupations; but in a post-industrial society it would appear to be an inadequate strategy, a producer of frail egos, agoraphobes, depressives, and millions of others whose condition in its baldest, most schematic state would seem to be represented by my passenger.

White Rabbit to the last, she left her gloves on the seat. But it was too late to call her back. And there was traffic backed up behind me, loudly complaining in a cacophony of klaxons that seemed to be shouting 'Off with his head! Off with his head!'

'Who cares for *you*,' I said. 'You're nothing but a pack of cars!' And I gave them the finger and pulled off.

From here, in flight over
the centre of the continent, it's easy to imagine oneself as an insect
in an art gallery, taking a slow, straight course above the surfaces
of a series of paintings by such artists as Lilly Sandover
Kngwarreye, Maxie Tjampitjinpa, Amy Johnson Jirwulurr
(especially her), and all their predecessors. From thirty thousand
feet the wilderness abstracts itself into the familiar configurations
and motifs of Aboriginal painting: wavelike formations, dap-
plings, dot clusters and textural patterns, serpentine curves,
tracklines, contourations.

Question: so how did those paleolithics get themselves up
this high? Aboriginal art is cartophiliac, and the view from this
plane is a cartophile's dream. Perhaps the answer is, too.

Below, the red heart is bathed in an acrylic glow. You can
almost smell it.

In the 1970s Aboriginals at Papunya west of Alice Springs
obtained contemporary synthetic media and canvas with which
to make their traditional narrative maps: this made the art both
more durable and more portable and, once expunged of ritual
secret detail, it was sold around the globe for big dollars. Thus
from the combination of ancient consciousness and modern
quick-drying luminous chemicals was born one of the world's
first post-civilised art movements, the 'Desert Acrylics'.[1] And

---

[1] Traffic flowing the other way – Western artists using prehistoric

that's what I'm looking down on from this aircraft window: a map of consciousness. A map which is also a territory.

I'm a cartophile, too. To track our route from Melbourne to Kuala Lumpur I've got a big, heavy relief map of Australia held up against the seatback. Just what does its shape represent? I see a bulging, halterneck brassière; Brigit sees a pair of old-but-spunky testicles. How fruitful, and how neat. Our companion in the aisle seat reckons we're made for each other. This man is by Greene out of Lowry. He wears a crumpled tropical suit and a yellowing Panama hat; he has a heavy stubble and a nose ravaged by spirits, and the archaeology of many meals is scattered across his shirtfront. A friendly chap, he has copies of the *Sydney Morning Herald* and *Granta* on his lap. The thinking man's Les Patterson. He's a doctor, and he's got himself a two-year stint making tax-free dollars in Kuwait. 'This sort of gig, it's like the French Foreign Legion, you know?' His wife is a Catholic. He left her last year, along with the kids and the iron. She won't divorce him, naturally. Now his girlfriend has left him, and he's been hitting the bottle a little strong. So – it's time for a *haj*.

'Radical way to dry out,' observed Brigit.

'I've only got one foot on the wagon,' he replies. 'And those fellers tolerate it if you're discreet.' A collection of little bottles on his tray table makes a kind of miniature dreaming. The wagon he mentions is obviously a dray.

The wrinkled warts of the McDonnell ranges are sweeping by below us as Dr Lowry-Greene asks Brigit how her visit has been.

---

materials, motifs and contexts – has swollen enormously since the Second World War, and has been intelligently (and lavishly) documented by Lucy Lippard in *Overlay* (Pantheon, New York, 1983). Lippard on mapping: 'It is a way of modernising the whole notion of art about space.'

'The worst times,' she says, 'were when it felt like living back at my parents' house in England, because that's all I used to hear when I was a kid – Australian voices. Well – one *big* Australian voice that drowned out the whole house – my Dad's. And around Sydney sometimes I'd have this nightmare, it was like all of Australia had turned into one enormous English semi, a giant 23 Bridge Road, and I couldn't get out of it, I was a helpless child. It was the voice. On the radio, on the street, at work, So this, now –' she waved around her and indicated the view from the window, '– feels like ten years ago when I first left home, for India, with my backpack, down the garden path. Only this time he's not standing in the doorway shouting after me, forbidding me to go and ordering me back. Crying too, he was.'

I glanced across the aisles to the movie screen. *North Shore Gothick* was playing, and Clarissa stood amongst the tombstones as she spoke:

'I am my father's favourite. This is why I am so pale.'

The Aboriginals seem to have little time for these blood relationships and their attendant pathos. As far as these peoples are concerned a child is an independent spirit who has merely chosen the mother to grow in of its own accord. They have been well aware of such things as paternity and the role of sperm, and probably were so long before the white man showed up – why else would their word for semen match the name of a fertility god? – it's just that these physiological facts have been of no social use to them. Born, a child's totem determines its 'spiritual' life, and it becomes part of an economic unit under all-encompassing tribal laws where every relationship is clearly defined along with its rights and obligations, and all relationships are accounted for. An individual's parents don't have much of a say in these matters, and no rights because of blood. If the natural father is not the mother's husband, no matter.

The sentiment attached by the West to biology is absent. (Similarly, Afro-Costa Rican children are regarded as belonging to the community as a whole.)

In the West, however, the wider networks of social bonding have completely atrophied, and been whittled down to a tiny unit based entirely on biology, and this unit itself is currently being atomised. Contemporary civilised families that do survive are held together with a strange glue of toxic drugs, domestic tyranny and public subsidy; while the wider social matrices where no rules apply and it's dog-eat-dog are wildly negotiated with desperate strategies of 'networking', attention- and approval-seeking, gladhanding and coercion.

Perhaps the prehistoric version is totalitarian; perhaps the civil version is inadequate and moribund. But would you rather be thought of as a free spirit or, as one civilised parent described her child on a TV show about education, your parents' 'most important investment'?

It is a strange, narcissistic fetish, this attraction of a gene to a copy of itself. Blood of my blood, fruit of my loins, mirror of mine . . . an autoerotic closed circuit. Of post-civilised kinship systems there is as yet no strong model, just a handful of experiments on early kibbutzim, in sixties China, and a string of small-scale communistic ventures. The squatting movement in Britain from the 1960s onwards produced some new versions of family/clan, as have the New Age Travellers, as has the fight for recognition of homosexual marriages and likewise the struggle to gain a degree of respect for solo parents. But in all these proto-societies the biological drug has been hard to kick and the familiar civil hierarchies often eventually reassert themselves. (The American Shakers are a peculiar exception: these communistics, founded in the eighteenth century and once populous, cared so little for the significance of reproductive chemistry that they are now down to single figures and have no qualms about their imminent demise.

175

They seem to have just got on with it and rejoiced in their own works, as Ecclesiastes has it, 'For who shall bring them to see what shall be after them?[2])

At what other points is the prehistoric world poking through the debris? What other plants are to be found on this bombsite? In our immediate vicinity there's *pituri*, of course – the shrub *Duboisia hopwoodii*, which when chewed in quids will ward off hunger, pain and fatigue – an Australian coca. But if the malaise goes deeper, something more like *Galbulimima belgraveana* may be required: a liquid decoction of the leaf and bark of this timber tree will have you encountering your archetypes in no time at all. They use this in Queensland and Papua New Guinea. But the entire globe is abloom with mind-expanding flora, whether you're in the Arctic taking reindeer urine laced with *Amanita muscaria*, doing psylocibin on Peckham Rye, peyote in Mexico or coleus in Brazil. And in the years since WWII the industrial world has been busy synthesising hallucinogens to meet its own growing demand, initially triggered by encounters between Western poets and ancient cultures. Shamanism too has spread beyond its paleolithic boundaries to the point where, along with universities offering degrees, practitioners can be found in most phone books.

One of the significant practices of shamanism which seems to have been overlooked by postwar experimenters in the West, both physicians and mavericks, is that in many traditional rituals of psychedelic healing it is the medicine-man (or woman) who takes the drug, not the client. The hallucinogen is neither analgesic nor disinfectant and makes no direct appeal to the immune system. Rather, it expands the healer's sensibilities in a way that enables him/her to perceive the client's

---

[2]*Ecclesiastes* 3: 22.

psychosomatic universe and to operate within an ecology of patient and healer. In the experiments of the last forty years there are examples a-plenty of mutual and group tripping and of individuals taking psychedelics whilst being monitored by a sober observer, but not of the more traditional practice, one which seems to make a lot of sense, especially in the context of mental or 'spiritual' problems: why, for example, give an already disturbed person sudden access to an intense and unfamiliar reality? It's not that some ghastly, damaging battle with demonic powers is necessarily bound to ensue, it's just that this method may be inappropriate. It may be that the patient is already well psychedelic – living in a world of voices and visions and archetypes – and more of the same clarifies nothing. Ordinary logical connections that the patient is asked to make or consider may not be forthcoming, viz. the military's experiments of the 1950s where bemused and irritated volunteers, high on large doses of LSD and alone in a room resembling a police cell, were asked by a disembodied voice to solve simple problems of arithmetic and could not cope at all. But what if the doctor is tripping and the patient is straight? The former, ideally an expert in familiar territory, with enhanced empathic and perceptual powers, may be of far better service in this situation.

It begins to resemble 'Physician, heal thyself.'

Brigit – in her savage aspect – suggests that psychiatrists be obliged to give themselves a quick hit of thorazine or ECT before consulting.

'Besides,' she says, 'it's nothing new. All doctors are junkies. I mean look at this archetype sitting next to me.'

Lowry-Greene is dozing in an analgesic, disinfected stupor. The oxblood brogue of his nose pokes out from under the brim of the tilted Panama hat.

Other medics with different poisons come to mind. The creations of Burroughs and Fassbinder, fixing up before entering their consulting rooms ... Freud's cocaine habit ... junior interns on 72-hour shifts bombed out on amphetamines ... the leather-elbowed family practitioner sucking on his pipe ... bored, pill-pushing GPs ... but our man here has the classic thaumaturge's tipple. Folklore has cast him in the same tragic-heroic mould as the war-weary soldier, for example:

> The siege had been raging for months with no sign of a let-up. Corpses were rotting in the streets. I found Dr Simon late one night in the bar of the Grand Hotel, on the first floor of which he had set up an improvised hospital. He sat in a corner, away from the flak-jacketed journalists, consular officials and black marketeers. He poured half the contents of a bottle of Glenfiddich into a pint glass, topped this up with water and then downed the lot in one protracted draught. I shivered inside. In all the time I had known him I had never dared approach the subject, but now I found myself saying quietly:
>
> 'Why, old chap? Why?'
>
> He lit a cigarette from the butt he had just smoked and looked up at me. I shall never forget those eyes, just as I shall never be able to describe them.
>
> 'My friend,' he said, 'if you had seen what these eyes have seen ...'[3]

and so forth. Or under canvas at MASH: Henry's filing cabinet stuffed with liquor, Hawkeye's domestic distillery.

Spirit alcohol is a very recent invention, being first recorded around the time of the fall of Rome. The rise of this toxic painkiller is strangely concurrent with the rise of Christendom and the violence of its assertion, as if the new empire had

---

[3] Graeme Malcolm, *Under the Heart of the Quiet Doctor* (Cape, London, 1965).

required the counter-invention of a deterrent. People used to speculate in the same way about LSD: discovered as the nuclear age dawned, was it the necessary antidote to the atomic bomb? (Both spirits and LSD are potentially destructive, but then so is a kiss.)

Lowry-Greene and his associates might conceivably, though clumsily, be on the right track. Before you engage with another's pain it helps to be pain-free yourself. This applies especially to ontological agonies. A post-civilised approach to psychotherapy would be for the therapist to take hallucinogens as a surgeon takes an X-ray, as a tool of vision. Imagine yourself depressed, confused, suicidal, awash with anxieties and illusions; and you have a choice of three medicine-persons. The first is an alcoholic who pays you a benumbed attention and offers you anti-depressants. The second is sober, the vast distance between you across the desktop is dry as a desert, his vision of you is utterly logical – paralysingly so, because your condition defies his logic; so he offers anti-depressants with the option of electricity at a later date. The third is tripped out on South American DMT, in all her Amazonic glory – you may not be aware of this, or you may catch a contact-euphoria and feel an almost physical strength to the encounter, but you won't be offered surgeries chemical, electrical or ectomic. Now, which of these three do you go for? If you ticked box (c), congratulations, you're truly post-civilised. Now try convincing the medical and political establishment of your preference. Despite the conspicuous failure of mainstream psychiatry, official research into psychedelic healing has been more or less closed down and criminalised for the past quarter-century. The field has been derelicted.

The desert below is now a hot, deep, luminous, rippling cyclamen pink, darkly dappled by shrubs. We appear to be riding the back of some gigantic, fabulous leopard.

*

Pre-civilised language is not literate. Perhaps they didn't have to deal with memorising the wealth of information generated by agricultural industry in terms of number and description. Sacks of corn, inventories. Or perhaps they had superior memories to ours today, and no need for writing. The ancient Greeks certainly had an art of memory that may well have been transmitted down through history to them; and, post-Gutenberg, Giordano Bruno attempted to revive it. He became Giordano Brûlé for his troubles.

No writing in pre-civilised days – they showed a picture, often a narrative map, and told its story, and acted it out. A Laurie Anderson performance. Essentially, a movie.

Because of movies, radio, TV, computers and telephones we are all becoming less literate. Literacy fights back with billboards. The chain-link fencing outside a school in Sydney's western suburbs is adorned with them – no ivory tower, this place. Less successfully, an office block in Oregon declares itself a 'Proffesional [sic] services plaza'. Big letters find their highest expression at the heart of big cities: SONY ... COKE ... SCHWARZENEGGER ... FIDEL, in a cluster of downtown neon, or proclamations chiselled into Assyrian walls. Look upon my works, ye mighty ...

Is the perennial objection to advertising and propaganda (especially in one's own backyard) a pre-civilised instinct, a resentment at the intrusion of literature into everyday life? The classic civil fantasy (often declared by *images* alone) is of a rural/suburban tranquillity, a place where there are no BIG LETTERS – no SHELL, no FREEDOM FOR/DEATH TO ... There are wealthier parts of the planet (Hampstead, Connecticut) where the big letters have been forced to shrink, often by those who own their meanings – the discreet McDonalds in a cosy clapboard village which may be populated by a number of big shareholders, etc.

But even the big billboards have recently begun to eschew words – Benetton, Benson & Hedges, and so forth. And there has been a revolution over the last thirty years where graphics have replaced letters. No more MAJOR ROAD AHEAD, LADIES' CLOAKROOM, NO SMOKING, TELEPHONE. This has made things a little quieter – you don't hear a pictogram. (In old-fashioned bicameral America you're still shouted at from across the street: WALK . . . DON'T WALK.)

Australians are in the aliterate vanguard. But they are also a vocal people, and they really know how to shout. Sydney is relatively free of neon valhallas like Times Square or Tokyo; it specialises in storefront barkers. Everywhere there are these hustlers stood on the sidewalk with mike and amplifier, calling you into drugstores, department stores, but most of all, and invariably, inviting you into the hundreds of outlets pushing surplus junk from the sweatshops of the Pacific Rim. These places make the discount palaces of Kilburn and Brixton – whose goods come from the same source – look puny. This *is* the Pacific Rim, brother, and we've more faulty backpacks, Chinese painting sets, brass knicknacks, cane chairs and Bart Simpson wristwatches than you could shake an incense stick at. Lately an air of recession-desperation has crept into the amplified spiel of women dressed like air stewardesses outside Soul Pattinson hyping reduced stacks of Brut and hairspray, and scousers (the men are invariably Liverpudlian boys) offering 80 per cent off a babydoll nightie: sometimes they will threaten you with the fact that they're closing down shortly. As if anyone cared. TV commercials here use the same technique: a guy in shirtsleeves stands in front of whatever he's selling – a cluster of cars, a pile of three-piece suites or stereos – and screams abuse at you in dollars.

The performance artist (theatre without text), the Aboriginal telling a story with the help of a painting, and the bozo with the sales pitch and the non-stick saucepan – it all amounts to the same post-civilised, pre-literate thing. Who needs writing? Accountants, lawyers – the people who invented it. And monotheist priests: the Jews with their revered scrolls, the sacred calligraphy of the Koran. Literature up till the time of the New Testament was a transcript of things uttered by poets and seers, propagandists and snake-doctors; from the Epic of Gilgamesh to the books of the prophets and the Song of Solomon. But by the time of St Paul, it has become Letters. Epistles, composed for the page. (The memory withers some more.) Hard to imagine some latter-day evangelist even being able to spell, let alone publish. Their medium is the video, their reading just sufficiently extensive to produce a handful of biblical soundbites. Writing may eventually die out because essentially it is too slow. Slower than thought, slower than speech, slower than a vision, slower than a poet. No one has time for it any more. It's enough trouble finding thought, speech, vision, poetry.

(And a decent non-stick saucepan, adds Brigit.)

We're now tracking the Daly River, south of Darwin, as it snakes its way through dense tropical forest towards Anson Bay on the Timor Sea: sudden shock of watercoloured grey-greens and saturated mustards.

They have named Darwin after the old evolutionary himself, although C.D. never came within two thousand miles of it. When he hit Sydney on the *Beagle* he was already knackered from five years at sea. He didn't stay in Australia long enough to see a single kangaroo. He spent all his time whingeing about the climate and the scenery. He took just six weeks to hop from Sydney to Hobart to King George's Sound in the west and left the continent with a two-fingered valediction trailing behind him like snot in the wind. This was the superbly patronising notion of Australia as a rising child too ambitious for affection and yet not big enough for respect. A statement loaded with implications of Oedipal fear and jealousy, and an attitude still around today in little old Great Britain. Taken on board by many Australians, at least in the back of their minds, it may well have helped crank up the cultural cringe that still lingers in places today.

Darwin didn't see kangaroos, but he saw Aboriginals do a roo dance. He may even have intuited that these people had beaten him to his world-shaking conclusions by several thousand years. Aboriginals theory holds that the first humans were transformations of animals. The conceptual architecture they raised around this basic hypothesis may differ in emphasis from that of the nineteenth-century avant-garde, but only slightly. If Darwin had used it he would merely have been described by his enemies not as an ape, but as a bearded witchetty grub, honey ant or wallaby. It's as if Darwin, in the true spirit of a jealous Victorian scientist, sensed a similar, rival theory holding sway down here and left quickly in a fit of pique.

The native Australians were also pretty hot on geology. As far as the birth of the earth is concerned they had none of those bizarre civil notions about sky gods snapping their fingers and *presto*. Paleolithic peoples were more aware of geological process (ideas just beginning to re-appear in Darwin's time through the work of Hutton and Lyell); they have ideas of emergence – from the ocean, from the rock, from orifices; and after the land come the people, from dung, from slime, from the kind of primal, fertile ooze of these coastal swamps that we're now leaving behind as we head out across the ocean.

It's been pointed out that civilisations may come and go, but certain pre-civilised peoples, so often nomadic, have survived for thousands of years to this day – and not necessarily by dint of hard work, either. Leisure played a large part in pre-civilised life. (In this context, Jesus' endorsement of the 'Lilies of the field' must have seemed startling to his – civilised – contemporaries. I don't know how all those protestant work ethicists deal with this one.) For post-industrial leisure, Australians are again in the vanguard. I consider all the contented, part-time lilies I met – Anna Nassauer, Vince McHugh (the Man with No History), Vicky, Colin Sutton, Phil Perkins – in the sitting position. This country is a part-timer's paradise. Consider too the worldwide revolution in personal mobility that has taken place this century, along with movements of vast populations of immigrants and refugees. These fluxes are certainly more radical than those which followed the fall of Rome, and it may be that only in archaic times have they been equalled. Today, most of us are neo-nomads.

We have left Australia behind, and crossed the Timor Sea, and are now flying over the islands that extend east from Java – Flores, Sumba, Lombok, Bali. Stretching away first to starboard, then to port, poking through the thick white cumulus, comes a string of volcano peaks, vast rims like the mouths of giant barnacles, shreds of cloud trailing off their slopes like the remains of some mucoid veil. These are the arseholes of creation, these are the Ancestors, bums up and turned to stone. We come closest to Old Man Sumbawa here, who has shat out his share of the East Indies and now lies sleeping, a lake of ice in the puckered crater of his anus. But for how long? Evening is falling, Lowry-Greene is dreaming of Mesopotamia, there are lights from domestic fires in the coastal villages below (stilted hut settlements niched between forest and sea), and I am left with this strange bouquet here on the tray table: the flowers of art, science, kinship, psychedelia, aliteracy, mobility, recreation, and others I don't recognise. Some are almost plastic; some are almost real. The string that binds their stalks has a card attached which says SNIFF ME. It's in Brigit's handwriting.